MW01253428

"As you read this boo
one you will feel sp
to the chapter you r
things that *matter*, how they influence the way we see and do
whether these moments are considered successful or opportunities
for growth. Finally, practical application examples are insightfully
accurate and practically useful for all."

    **—Charles Wells,** Texas high school baseball coach

"This book is a must-read for athletes and their parents. Providing
practical, ready-to-use advice on how to navigate today's high-stakes
competition landscape, this book helps readers get all that is intended
out of their sport and survive, and thrive in, the journey. You can
smell the coffee being made as you read."

    **—Damon West,** keynote speaker and best-selling author of *The Coffee Bean: A Simple Lesson to Create Positive Change*

"The words within are mindfully crafted armor against damaging
blows for athletes and those who raise them. Reading it will cause
growth, and implementing the ideas will improve all who interact
with athletes. This book should be required reading for anyone who
wants to compete."

    **—Dr. Andy Laughlin,** NCAA Faculty Athletic Representative

"Dr. Fraze is a huge part of our program because he brings a unique
and impactful perspective on character development and leadership.
His passion is clear, and his message is priceless to the young men and
women who get the chance to hear it."

    **—Danny McCray,** Director of Youth Camps at The Dallas Cowboys

"This book meets head on the craziness that is destroying the original
intent of athletics. It provides ready-to-use suggestions for helping
both athletes and parents get the most out of athletics. A must-read!"

    **—Larry Hays,** head softball coach at Colorado Christian University, College Hall of Fame baseball coach

"This book is a great resource and must-read for athletes and their
families."

    **—Jon Gordon,** 15x best-selling author of *The Energy Bus* and *Training Camp*, JonGordon.com

"This meticulously and skillfully authored book offers practical, relevant, applicable, biblically based wisdom to student-athletes, coaches, parents, and supporters seeking to better understand and navigate the complex and demanding world of competitive athletics."

    —**Cory S. Powell,** MA, Senior Director, Texas Tech University, University Interscholastic League

"I've known Monica for close to 25 years. During her time as a competitive athlete, she had many obstacles to work through. The way she was able to handle adversity during that time set the groundwork for where her career is today. She understands the athlete and the many scenarios that may arise during training, practice, and games. Her understanding of the athlete is what separates her from the rest of the people in her field. The different modalities she uses to help student-athletes are derived from her time as an athlete. That is a rarity in this field—the ability to use past athletic experiences to help other athletes perform at their best."

    —**Aaron Uzzell,** Master Strength and Conditioning Coach, former NCAA DI Texas Tech University S&C coach, current Frenship Athletics 6A S&C coach

"David Fraze changed our team and, thereby, my life. He is an expert on kids and sports culture, and he has not only academic knowledge but proven skill in implementing what it takes to build great sports teams and families. Anything he writes, I read, then apply, so my team and my family can be better."

    —**Ged Kates,** head football coach, athletic coordinator, Richland High School

"David Fraze is a steadfast and integral part of our football program. He has been the catalyst in intentionally shaping the culture and chemistry of our team and building confidence and self-assurance in our athletes. He is an expert in his field, building and creating relationships with a team and the individuals within. He makes everyone around him better!"

    —**Jay Northcutt,** head football coach, boys athletic coordinator, Frenship High School

# PRACTICAL WISDOM

## FOR *FAMILIES* WITH *ATHLETES*

# PRACTICAL WISDOM

## FOR *FAMILIES* WITH *ATHLETES*

### WINNING ISN'T THE ULTIMATE GOAL

## DAVID FRAZE & MONICA WILLIAMS

LEAFWOOD
PUBLISHERS
an imprint of Abilene Christian University Press

# PRACTICAL WISDOM FOR FAMILIES WITH ATHLETES
*Winning Isn't the Ultimate Goal*

L E A F W O O D
P U B L I S H E R S
*an imprint of Abilene Christian University Press*

Copyright © 2024 by David Fraze and Monica Williams

ISBN 978-1-68426-003-4

Printed in the United States of America

Cataloging-in-Publication Data is on file at the Library of Congress, Washington, DC.

Cover design by Greg Jackson, Thinkpen Design
Interior text design by Sandy Armstrong, Strong Design

Leafwood Publishers is an imprint of Abilene Christian University Press.
ACU Box 29138
Abilene, Texas 79699

1-877-816-4455
www.leafwoodpublishers.com

24  25  26  27  28  29  30  //  7  6  5  4  3  2  1

To Lisa, there are not enough words to express my love for you and the joy of being your husband. I totally outkicked my coverage when you said, "Yes!" You are an incredible, talented, and wise woman.

To my family, thank you for loving, supporting, and participating in my work with competitive athletics. You get it.

To the coaches whose words resonate in my mind to this day. I pray your above-average impact in the life of an average athlete will be seen in the pages of this book. Thank you.

To the athletes, athletic families, and coaches who work to navigate the world of athletics with faith and family prioritized. This book is for all of us.

To the starting offensive and defensive linemen and coaches of the 2023 edition of the Frenship Tigers. As a coach, I spend most of my time with the boys in the trenches. Outside those who "know," if you do your job, you don't get the credit you deserve; if you don't do your job, you receive the blame. Your names are in a book. I would go to battle with you guys any day. OL coaches: Chris Fanelli and Wes Havens; OL: Greyson Pelsor, Saul Trevino, Grayson Page, Eli Hicks, Jake Sowder, and Brooks Franklin. DL coaches: Dusty Robinson and Noel Ramos; DL: Caden Spano, Estavan Aguilar, Jacob Bankston, and Mederrick Harper.

David

To my family, especially my "Little People." Soraya and Asher, "we are called to leave an inheritance for our children." When God calls me to a project like this book, I am confident that God will use it for his glory and to add to your inheritance. To Mom, Dad, Jerome, Amelia, Trinity, and Jayden. Your love covers me. It enables me to move faster and rise higher. Thank you for loving me. To Deac, thank you for the conversations that resulted in a few chapters beginning or ending with something you shared. To the countless families, friends, athletes, and coaches who chose to do competitive sport the "right way." Thank you, because any time you choose right in sport, that is a narrow road. Blessings to all who supported this effort and to all who will read it.

Now, specifically to athletes:

I also dedicate this book to you athletes. You initially engaged in sport to have fun with friends and as an outlet for self-expression. The nature of competition—to win—causes many involved in competitive sport to drift from fun and self-expression to hyper-identifying as athletes, essentially foreclosing identity exploration. I encourage you—the athlete—to bring your full self to the sport. Refuse to be one-dimensional. Develop other interests and other aspects of your identity. You will find that all of you is needed to be the best you, even in your field of play. Play hard, have fun, and when it is time, know you can walk away from sport thankful for the experiences and opportunities it afforded you.

Monica

"Play for the love of the game. For the fun. For the thrill of victory and the agony of defeat. Not to get a scholarship, or make the All-City or All-State Team, or even be 'The Starter' on your team. Play to get all the wonderful experiences and emotions only Sport can give you. Play so you can feel alive!"

—M. A. Ribaudo

# CONTENTS

Foreword, by Stephen Mackey................................................... 13

Preface ............................................................................. 19

Acknowledgments ................................................................ 23

Introduction....................................................................... 25

Balance Matters................................................................... 31

Coaching Matters ................................................................ 39

Conflict Matters .................................................................. 51

Failure Matters ................................................................... 63

Fun Matters........................................................................ 75

Identity Matters .................................................................. 83

Mindset Matters................................................................... 91

Parenting Matters................................................................ 103

Reality Matters ................................................................... 111

Responsibility Matters .......................................................... 121

Strength and Conditioning Matters............................................ 129

Transition Matters ............................................................... 139

Church Matters.................................................................... 147

Conclusion ........................................................................ 157

    In Their Own Words ......................................................... 159

    Student Athlete Words of Wisdom ....................................... 169

    How to Be a Good Fan...................................................... 175

    Rules for Parents and Athletic Families................................... 179

    Five Things to Know before Playing Football ........................... 183

    Helpful Verses for Athletes and Families ............................... 191

    Helpful Resources........................................................... 193

Notes ............................................................................... 197

# FOREWORD

No matter how you look at it, it's not hard to see that sports matter.
Professional sports account for billions of dollars of revenue every year, and some of the biggest icons in the world are sports figures. At the collegiate level, billions of dollars are spent every year on NCAA athletics, and an athletic scholarship, for many, is a "golden ticket." There are 15 million high school students in America, and over half of them participate in some form of sport or athletic competition.

So it's no wonder that young people and their parents are choosing to rearrange their lives, their schedules, and their values for youth sports—what wouldn't a parent do to give their kid a shot at the next level? Families spend exorbitant amounts of money on personal trainers and exclusive travel teams in the hopes of giving their kids an edge toward social standing, a college scholarship, or a professional sports career.

While you might think parents who are part of a faith community would view athletics as a lesser priority than participation in their local church, you'd be wrong. One of the primary obstacles to faith formation given by youth ministers is participation in, and the busyness that comes from, athletic competitions and extracurricular activities. (Let's face it: it is really hard for a youth minister's Wednesday or Sunday night program to "compete" with the perceived scarcity of opportunities for young people to reach their goals or become professional athletes.) The "win-at-all-costs" mentality that is synonymous with athletics seems incompatible with the Christian ethic at best, and grossly perverts it into something Jesus would never recognize at its worst. The striking similarities between athletic competition and idolatry are hard to miss.

However, the number of student-athletes who will earn a college scholarship is depressingly low, and the number who make it to the pros is even smaller. Which is why it is so dangerous that so many student-athletes find their identity, value, and worth in their athletic performance. Sports will end. For every athlete. Either by choice (their own or a coach's), circumstance (something outside their control), or by competition (they aren't talented enough to advance).

What then?

What are kids to do—having been taught, implicitly or explicitly, that the sum total of their identity is to be an athlete, or that their worth is determined by their performance—when sports are taken away? Sadly, many will turn to harmful practices, others will get depressed and feel lost, and all too often, they will take their own lives. The destruction that can come when a young person finds their hope, identity, and purpose in sports, only to have it taken away by injury, insufficiency, or bad luck, is heartbreaking.

But what if it didn't have to be this way? What if it were possible for athletic competition to be more than a one-way street to disengagement? What if the classroom of athletics could be spiritually formative, socially positive, and actually help strengthen the relationship between student-athletes and God, and their family?

Not only do I believe it is possible, I believe this book offers up a game plan for parents, coaches, youth ministers, and student-athletes to follow so that athletics can do more than fill their schedules—it can be a discipleship tool to help them fill their hearts.

How, you ask? By connecting the dots between sports, life, and our faith; by helping us see what really matters.

In her book *Saying Is Believing*, Amanda Drury wrote, "[Adults] do not and cannot force the presence of God. They can, however, help train the eyes of teenagers to be aware of God's presence."

I know well the transformative power of this statement.

As a high school senior, I was torn between the influence I could have on the football team as a captain and the sporadic nature in which I could participate in youth group activities during the season. When I met with my youth minister, however, he didn't counsel me to quit football.

Instead of asking me to quit the team because that limited my participation in youth group activities, he took the time to teach me to make the game of football an act of worship, challenged me to make the football team my mission field, and encouraged me to live like Jesus would in the locker room. No agenda or language that suggested the most faithful execution of those things meant I brought my friends to church. Just a hyperintentional investment in identifying the most helpful next step in my faith journey—and equipping me to take it.

In short, rather than competing with sports for my attention or time, he met me where I was and "trained my eyes" to see God and the opportunity for "God moments" in the context of sports. That year, twelve of my teammates gave their lives to

Jesus and dozens of others got involved in the team Bible study he helped prepare me to lead.

That season changed my life.

The practical wisdom in this book will not "force the presence of God" on you, your student athlete, or their coach. What it can do, however, is help "train your eyes" to see how in the small, seemingly insignificant moments of sport, God is present.

When you are overwhelmed with practice: God is present.

When you are angry at your coach: God is present.

When you fall short and lose: God is present.

When you win: God is present.

When you have tough decisions to make: God is present.

When you feel the pressure of performance: God is present.

When you don't make the team: God is present.

When you are focused on a big goal: God is present.

When you get hurt: God is present.

When you are finished playing sports: God is present.

This is not just good news for those who claim to follow Jesus; this is good news for everyone. Why? Because it means there is more to sports than meets the eye. When you dare to see "beyond the game," you will see that the classroom of athletics can be one that gives you tools to compete in sports and life; that will build a strength of character that can overcome opponents on the field and adversity in life; that in sports, and in life, there is something bigger at play.

I know there is so much that can happen and go wrong in athletic competition, but that's kind of the point. Sports are life and leadership at lightspeed; they are real life. Things go wrong in real life, and students need to be equipped to see that there is more at play than just this moment—that there is a real God who is really present in every moment and is really for them. When we expand our imagination to see sports as a location of faith formation, we can help students see God in sports and in their lives.

My prayer for you as you read through the pages of this book is that you would have the eyes to see: God is with you. God is present.

And that is what *really* matters.

Stephen Mackey
Player Development Coach, and *Wall Street Journal* best-selling author of *The Locker Room: How Great Teams Heal Hurts, Overcome Adversity, and Build Unity*

# PREFACE

Thank you for picking up our book. We hope you find the content helpful, challenging, practical, and enjoyable to read. There are things you need to know before reading this book. This book cannot . . .

* make your athlete a superstar (but it can help them become the best version of themselves).
* make your athlete's difficult team environment better (but you and your athlete can better understand how to navigate such situations).

What this book can do is . . .

* help families navigate the world of competitive athletics.
* help families get the most out of competitive athletics.
* help families manage the expectations and realities of competitive athletics.
* help families survive and thrive in the journey through competitive athletics.

We are writing from a place of deep respect and love for your family, athlete, and sport. Our words come from our experience and scholarship and represent an extension of sharing one another's burdens. We use Scripture to support and supplement our experience and scholarship. We are not preaching at you nor performing a bait and switch (stop and Google that if you haven't heard that term) on our audience. You did not pick up a "Bible book." Our use of Scripture is an attempt to be transparent and authentic as authors.

As with any writing project, tough decisions on content have to be made. The decisions on what to include in this book came down to content that highlights frequently asked questions and topics the authors field from parents, coaches, and athletes regarding how to navigate sports, especially competitive sports.

## WHY THIS BOOK IS INCLUDED IN A SERIES ON YOUTH MINISTRY

In the twenty-first century, the field of youth ministry has left its organizational adolescence and entered young adulthood. It has become more sophisticated. The world has changed. Families have changed . . . culture has changed . . . the journey into adulthood has changed. Things. Have. Changed. However, many parents and leaders operate from a sentimental view of their own adolescent experience. The change, and corresponding stress and pressure placed on students and parents, is seen in the world of competitive athletics.

What has emerged from the youth ministry trenches is a loud cry for more. More adult mentors significantly integrated in teens' lives. More adult mentors offering emotional and spiritual support. More adult mentors offering relational authenticity. More adults being present in what God is already doing in our youth ministries.

The stress on families and students created by participation in competitive athletics has created the same cry for "more" from youth workers, families, and athletes. *Practical Wisdom for Families with Athletes* is that resource families have been looking for to help them *survive, thrive,* and *enjoy* the journey through competitive athletics. This book in the Practical Wisdom series represents the research and proven methods the authors present to parents, coaches, administrators, and athletes on a regular basis. It is the desire of the authors that this book proactively supports and nurtures families who are trying to balance competitive athletics with identity, character, and spiritual development in their student athlete.

## HOW TO READ THIS BOOK

All new appliances, computers, televisions, phones, power tools, gaming systems, and assembly-required furniture come with a full set of instructions for setup and use. However, because we are impatient and ready to use our purchase quickly, most of these come with a one-page, easy-to-understand set of quick start-up instructions.

I like the quick start-up instructions. Depending on the complexity of the start-up, most instruction guides are one to four pages max. The steps are easy to follow and filled with valuable information, and they typically let you know when you are out of your league and need to open up the complete set of instructions.

The book you are holding is a quick-start guide for athletic families and the third book in the Practical Wisdom series. Depending on the complexity of the topic, most chapters are concise. The steps are easy to follow and are sandwiched between actual playing, coaching, or consulting stories that highlight the need for and application of the truth being discussed. The information is arranged in three parts:

 **Why:** Professional and theological underpinnings and support for the truth

 **How:** Practical application and discussion of the truth

 **Now:** First-steps suggestions for strengthening the truth or making the truth a part of your participation in competitive athletics

Helpful endnotes are provided for clarification and deeper study. The endmatter contains information that is too good to leave out of the book. In short, there is no "right way" to read this book. You can read front to back or skip around to the topic you need quick start-up assistance with right now.

Wherever you start, thank you for allowing us to join your family in your journey through competitive athletics. We are humbled and honored with the trust you have given.

Monica and David

# ACKNOWLEDGMENTS

"Monica, when are you and Dr. Fraze going to write a book?" Those words, spoken by Dr. Bridgette Hester, Dr. Williams's dissertation chair, were the push we needed to get our idea off the ground and into your hands. There are a host of people we want to acknowledge and honor for their help in completing this book.

> *"Whatever you do, whether in word or deed,*
> *do it all in the name of the Lord Jesus,*
> *giving thanks to God the Father through him."*
> —Paul the apostle (Col. 3:17)

We are Christ followers. As such, all we do and all we are is first and foremost a reflection of our devotion to the Lord Jesus. All of it. We acknowledge the Lord's impact in our personal and professional lives.

> *"A coach will impact more people in one year than the*
> *average person will in an entire lifetime."*
> —Billy Graham

We have played, coached, and trained athletes as individuals and part of a team. As you will see, these experiences have impacted, and continue to impact, our lives deeply. The time and sacrifice coaches give to their athletes, teams, and sport is often misunderstood, underappreciated, and difficult to explain to others. As is often heard among coaches, "You know if you know." *We know* and acknowledge the impact you are making in the lives of athletes on and off the field of competition. We dare not start a list of those we have been coached by and we have coached with. (We are sitting in a coffee shop trying to figure out how to mention each of you; we just can't because we don't know where to begin to express our love and appreciation for you all.) We do hope you find your impact in the pages of this book, and many of your voices are heard in the endmatter.

> *"A life is not important except*
> *in the impact it has on other lives."*
> —Jackie Robinson

The athletes we have worked with and continue to work with are special. They are *our* people, family. The lessons learned from our experiences together are numerous and go both ways. When we are at the end of our days, we will think back to you and smile.

To our colleagues at Lubbock Christian University, we acknowledge the support and space you give us to work on this book and share our time with athletes and teams across the country.

Jason Fikes, Duane Anderson, and the team at Leafwood continue to support and believe in the value of the Practical Wisdom series of books. Thank you for your continued dedication to resourcing youth ministry, families, and the church. Your impact is eternal.

# INTRODUCTION

Michael Phelps was the winningest athlete in Olympic history, earning twenty-three gold medals. I stumbled across an ESPN interview that did not celebrate Michael's wins. It was a candid conversation where Phelps described himself as a "train wreck" with "low self-esteem" outside of the pool.[1] Phelps lost himself in competitive sport. Family and friends like his wife and Ray Lewis, former safety for the NFL Baltimore Ravens, had to remind him that he was so much more than the athlete he portrayed. Now with a newly realized identity and worth, Phelps says, "I am just me."

Phelps reminds us that athletes are "human" and not "action figures." Phelps is not alone in his public advocacy for mental illness. Kevin Love, the center-forward for the Cleveland Cavaliers, echoes Phelps's struggles with mental illness and calls others to seek help.[2] Unfortunately, these are not isolated incidents in sport. Consider Simone Biles, who pulled out of the 2020 Tokyo Olympics, citing mental health issues that were "too much."[3] Competitive athletes feel the pressure but often deal with it in isolation.

Popular wisdom for competitive athletics and proponents for sports tout the physical, mental, and social benefits of athletics. Mantras like, "Learn to play sports well to do life well," bolster arguments for athletic participation. These positions are true in many cases, but they are also shortsighted and do not acknowledge the physical, mental, and social risks associated with competitive sports.

A few years ago, I entered the world of mental performance coaching. Not from a desire to "counsel" people but out of necessity, because I understand the consequences for people who lose themselves and their identity to sport, namely competitive sport. I have experienced in my personal life and witnessed in my work with athletes the highs and lows of athletics: the highs related to personal and corporate wins; the lows among people who fail to use sport as a mechanism to learn practical life lessons, like how to win humbly, regroup from failure, stay disciplined, be committed, invest in a team, and remain grateful as an athlete. The changing landscape of contemporary athletics requires parents, coaches, and athletes to attend to what it now means to be an *athlete*.

## CHANGE OF CONTEMPORARY SPORT

Traditionally, participation in athletics was about effort over outcome, teamwork above individualization, and access versus select. Conventional definitions for athletics no longer hold where individuals, even young athletes, are now relegated to performers with most of the feedback they receive focused on performing and not personal spiritual growth and emotional well-being. Hence, the dark side of being a competitive athlete due to the nature of competition—to win.

Does this sound familiar, "All I do is win, win, win, no matter what"?[4] I hear these seemingly innocent lyrics and have been guilty of singing them myself. Now think about the lyrics in the context of what it means to be a competitive athlete, particularly the "no matter what" part.

Competitive sport speaks to an end—to win. The premium placed on winning compels athletes to engage in attitudes and behaviors that net that end—to win no matter what—to the point that identity investment in practices that provide a competitive advantage becomes and remains the focus to the detriment of other identity formation practices. Parents and coaches of competitive athletes must guard against tendencies to make sports about winning and talent development instead of keeping sports athlete-centric and using them to help teach life lessons, even spiritual formation, which is hard to do with the time competitive athletics requires. Sports cannot effectively teach what parents do not value.

The current competitive sports landscape takes an all-in approach, leaving little to no middle ground for recreational play versus select or club play. I asked my colleague and friend Dr. Chris Huggins, the father of a budding competitive athlete, about his take on sports. Chris mentioned the fight for middle ground in sports, especially at the youth sports level. Chris's athlete is "too athletic" for recreational sports, and his family refuses to construct their lives around involvement in select or club teams.

To Dr. Huggins's point, athletic families are largely willing to build schedules and allocate resources around the demands of competitive sports. Those demands often siphon time from other family activities and strain finances. Parents and athletes feel the pressure to accommodate select and club practice and travel schedules that tax the family so that participation becomes the primary social construct—*it is what our family does and largely who we are.*

As authors, Dr. David Fraze and I felt the tug to distill years of experience in sports and hundreds of conversations with parents, coaches, and athletes into one easy-to-read quick-start guide. This book is not about how to build a super athlete. Quite the opposite, this book is about how to not destroy the person in the athlete. As one of our student athletes Megan Mirabal, LCU Women's Soccer goalkeeper, put it:

> Parents and coaches need to realize we are already hard on ourselves, so they need to know it cannot be all pressure all the time. We want to please our parents and coaches, and we think only focusing on our sport is the way to make them happy. It took my parents sitting me down and telling me that they were happy with me as a person and not as an athlete for me to get it.

## TRUTH MATTERS

*Practical Wisdom for Families with Athletes* intends to invite parents, coaches, and athletes into deeper conversations about the nature of their relationship with competitive athletics. This book requires truth. Readers will locate themselves in some of the chapters.

Locating ourselves in the pages of this book is great, but not enough. The next step is to make course corrections, which require truth that leads to action. Competitive athletics is not the issue. The issue is the unwillingness of those affiliated with competitive sports to identify and address the dark side of sports. We have an opportunity to do something meaningful and to challenge the all-in, identity-robbing practices in sports so athletes can do what they were initially recruited to do: "Have fun with friends!"

The stakes are too high not to take to heart why identity, parenting, responsibility, and the other topics covered in this book matter. Unfortunately, Dr. Fraze and I end up running postmortems on programs and approaches that have damaged competitive athletes because they did not recognize there was a person tethered to the athlete. I realize as I write this introduction that some might be convicted by the opening paragraphs and be tempted to stop reading. If that is you, David and I trust that God will do something with the "mustard seed" that compelled you to read the introduction. For those of you willing to keep reading, let's get to work.

# BALANCE
# MATTERS

"There is no decision that we can make that doesn't
come with some sort of balance or sacrifice."

—Simon Sinek

"Our son wants to go to summer camp, but his select team
needs him to pitch both weekends in each big weekend series.
Your travel plans eliminate him from both games." This was
the problem the parent, a committed church member and volunteer, communicated to me when the dates for camp were
announced. This man's son was a legit, next-level baseball
player. He had already received offers and would be receiv-
ing more in the coming months. The dilemma was real to this
young man's future in baseball and education. The math was
simple: missing both games communicated a lack of dedication
to team and sport and could throw up red flags to interested
college coaches. Playing in both games communicated, for this

family, a shift in priorities and would hinder their son's faith development. Sound like a familiar tension?

**Balance matters.**

## WHY?

It is possible that the above story created a bit of angst in you. Why? Because the challenge of finding balance between competitive athletics and other growth opportunities (e.g., camps, mission trips, other non-sport extracurriculars, family vacations, worship, etc.) is real. In the past, balance was easier to come by because Sundays and Wednesdays were off limits for games and practice. In today's athletic world, these days are no longer sacred.[1] Actually, balance is essential for all parts of life.

### The World Was Created in Balance

Coming from a Christian worldview, the first chapters of the Bible tell the story of a God who prepares a balanced environment that can sustain life and promote growth and flourishing. The most casual of readers can see the creation of a world in balance. In other parts of Scripture, the divine balance of creation is held up against the chaos created by a world corrupted by deception and sin.

One of my favorite *balance versus chaos* sections of Scripture comes from the book of Job and the response the Lord gives to the chaos (lack of balance) lamented by Job. What was Job concerned about? Suffering. He experienced a lot of that in his lifetime and decided to ask God, "What's up with all the trouble?" And . . . God actually answers Job. God begins his response with "Who is this that obscures my plans with words without knowledge? Brace yourself like a man; I will question you, and you shall answer me" (Job 38:2–7). God concludes with an impressive retelling of how the world he created was balanced and in working order and the angels applauded his work. Applauded!

What I want you to notice is that the unbalance (chaos) Job experienced was not because the Lord created a world out of balance. Another of my favorite *balance versus chaos* sections of Scripture comes from the apostle Paul (a big deal among early Christian leaders; I am sure you have heard his name; he wrote a lot of stuff in the Bible). He wrote to his Roman readers that the "frustrated" balance of creation, witnessed in the "bondage to decay," is encouragement to people "frustrated" by their own unbalance amid suffering and pain. In short, as spring comes after winter, so will a spring-like, hopeful outcome come after the present chaotic winter of suffering (Rom. 8:18–23). The point is clear: even in our chaotic state, caused by either the way we live or outside forces, God's desire for his creation is to be in balance.

Amid today's high-stakes, constant-pace, competitive athletic environment, I am finding more and more athletes saying things like . . .

"I need some rest!"

"I need a weekend to do something other than travel to another game!"

"I can't get _____ done!"

"I can't keep up with everything!"

"I'm thinking about quitting."

"I am just angry all the time."

There are many more of these types of statements, and all point to the fact that the world of today's athlete and athletic family can quickly drift out of balance and into chaos without focused intentionality.

## God Created a Pattern of Balance for Humanity

Recently, I (David) had the chance to visit the Muslim country Jordan. On Friday afternoons, the very busy city I was in would slow down to a crawl. Why? It is a practice of their faith to take a break and rest. Why? Balance! Most cultures take time and have a weekly pattern intended to restore *balance*. Hmmm?

If I had a dollar for every time I have said, or have heard someone else say, "I don't need a day off," I would be a wealthy man. The truth is, whether we acknowledge it or not, we were not built for running ourselves into the ground. We need rest, balance. The God of the Bible demonstrated a pattern of balance in the first chapters of Genesis. Another familiar story: God created the world in six days and then rested on the seventh day. To be clear, I am pretty sure God was not "tired" (maybe), but it does seem he wanted to step back and take a moment to enjoy his work (Gen. 2:1–2). This modeling by the Creator would become a practice of Sabbath by his creation. It was not a day of "worship"; it was a day of "rest."[2] Why? Without rest, humans fall out of balance. We see no need to illustrate this truth because most of those involved in competitive athletics often talk of busy schedules, lost weekends, and exhausted athletes.

## Competitive Athletes Recognize the Need for Balance in Competition

As talked about in the chapter "Strength and Conditioning Matters," physical and mental balance are imperative to getting the most out of your athlete's competitive ability. Still, because of many common fears (failure, missing an opportunity, falling behind, wasting money, etc.), today's athletes are sustaining injuries from their lack of balance. They are pushing their overworked, overstressed, and overgamed (that's not a word) bodies into game-ending, season-ending, and career-ending injuries.[3] Athletic trainers, strength and conditioning coaches, and other coaching professionals are constantly preaching the message of balance. They caution their athletes on the dangers (physical and mental) of constant training and competition. In short, competitive athletes need to embrace and protect balance. That is easier said than done in today's competitive environment. However, balance is possible.

 ## HOW?

I am sure you and your student athlete feel the pressure involved in competitive athletics. That is a good thing and will keep an athlete motivated and striving toward excellence. But it can quickly devolve into an out-of-balance life. Here are a few suggestions for keeping performance high and balance a reality.

### Listen to the Professionals

Today's athlete has tremendous resources to draw from. Trainers, strength and conditioning staffs, and coaches are equipped with the latest methods for training and motivating athletes. Yes, as mentioned throughout this book, there are coaches who overlook training and best practices to get the win. We believe most coaches (especially those involved with school-based teams) care about winning and their athletes. Consult these professionals when your student is being approached by an outside team, performance program, or elite camp opportunity. They will give you their honest opinion of how each of these opportunities will help, hurt, or hinder your athlete. Furthermore, most professional coaches will have already stated their balance ideals in a season orientation meeting. Trust your professional resources.

### Listen to Your Athlete

This one is tough. As an athletic family involved in the grind of competition, you understand the difficult balance of knowing whether your athlete needs her work ethic checked or whether she needs a break. Either way, listen to your athlete and let them help define their level of balance. With that said, and I say this strongly, you are the adult. It is possible your student athlete needs more balance, and they don't recognize that need. Be. The. Adult.

### Choose Select Teams and Elite Training Opportunities Carefully

This one hits personally for both Monica and me. Why? We have seen such programs manipulate athletic families for personal exposure and profit. It is true, such programs can be of great benefit and encouragement; others create opportunities for injury and will throw balance off quickly. How do you know? Consult the professionals mentioned above. They know what is and what is not worth your time and money.

### Trust Your Gut and Resist Pressured, Fear-Based Decisions

Regardless of the practical insight provided thus far, families continue to disregard all of it and end up in an unbalanced situation. Why? Because they ignore their gut, feel pressured by other adults or athletes, and react in fear that they will miss out on something. Fight this urge and trust yourself. Again: Be. The. Adult.

### Practice and Model Balance in All Areas of Your Life

We are talking athletics in this book. However, if you really want to establish balance in your athletic family, establish balance in all areas of your family life. Is there an area of your life out of balance (e.g., work, technology, hobby, etc.)? Get it in balance.

This will give you practice, and credibility, to establish more balance in your athlete's life.

### Abide by or Create Off-Season Opportunities

There are seasons in competitive athletics. However, in today's competitive environment, it is possible to play your sport all year round. Be careful. This will not be the best for your family or athlete and may lead to burn out or injury.[4] Again, consult a professional before jumping into "extra season" opportunities.

 **NOW?**

It is possible you are reading this chapter first because you know things are out of balance in your athletic family. If that is the case, it may be difficult to find an off-ramp from your current out-of-balance situation. Off-ramps could be the end of a season, end of a tournament, or end of a training session in which an intentional break is scheduled for your athlete. In Texas, the governing body of athletic competition, UIL (University Interscholastic League), creates moments in the year's competition calendar in which no practice or UIL-sanctioned competition can occur without penalty. If your state creates such moments, don't fill these with non-sanctioned athletic activity. Rest and find some balance.

If you are starting your journey through competitive athletics, commit now to practicing a few of the balance-producing suggestions given. You will be glad you started with balance in mind.

Strong in sport and stronger in faith commitment, the family found a solution to the camp travel versus elite select baseball game problem. They worked with the coach to determine when their son was scheduled to pitch in the rotation and drove their son to camp themselves after his final pitch. Arriving late on the first night, the athlete missed nothing of camp. The family returned to camp on the last night, left after the final wrap-up, and took their elite athlete to that weekend's series. The camp was in central New Mexico, and our church was in Fort Worth! A lot of driving. A window for a lot of "What happened at camp?" time—priceless. A lot of sleeping and rest. Balance modeled, defended, and experienced. It may take a bit of creativity, but it is worth it.

**Balance matters.**

# COACHING
# MATTERS

"The key to coaching is love. It's not knowledge; it's not discipline. If you love 'em, you can discipline them. If you love 'em, you can yell at them and laugh about it later."

—Dabo Swinney

## A tale of two coaches.

"*You are not starting on defense this week.*" I was a two-way starter, showed potential to play at the next level, and I was being benched by my coach?! He had called me into the hallway to tell me the news. Before he dropped the news, Coach explained that he had talked to my previous coaches about what he was witnessing in my midseason play and practice. I had a problem of coasting and going through the motions, not giving my best effort. My other coaches validated his conclusion and witnessed the same drop in performance. It was one of the most influential moments of my young life; *it changed me.* I eventually won back my starting position on defense, but the true victory was life change created by a coach who cared about my play and for me as a young man in need of coaching. It may be obnoxious to those closest to me, but since that moment, I don't let up on any project, from mowing yards to cleaning the garage, until it is finished. Why? I was benched in tenth grade.

"*I trust you and will not hesitate to play you!*" These were the words my first-year varsity head coach spoke to me in private and in public to the team. I was part of a truly sensational defensive front that featured my friend John. John was going to progress to the NCAA Division I level. I, on the other hand, was going to a school without a football program to pursue a degree in youth ministry. I knew my place and role. I also realized my playing days would, more than likely, end at the end of the season. With that said, we had a wonderful rotation of four that was effective and rested key players. Here was the problem: for whatever reason, toward the end of the season, my defensive line coach had to fight with the head coach to keep me in the starting rotation on game day and practice. After several telling incidents, it was obvious—my coach had *lied* to me and had no intention of playing me without conflict. I was certainly not the only player he had treated this way, but I was one of them; and it caused damage. To this day, even though I have worked through the pain of that season, I remember and fight the urge to associate my accomplishments with my value as a person.

A tale of two coaches. One cultivated confidence. One cultivated doubt.

**Coaching matters.**

 ## WHY?

I have not met an athlete who did not *want* a coach or to be coached. To qualify, I have met several athletes and families that did not know how to accept coaching or did not agree with a coach's decisions or philosophy (these situations will be discussed later in the chapter). For now, the truth is, we all want and desire good coaches in our lives. I want to flex my theological muscles again and give you a few biblical examples of coaching. These chosen examples demonstrate the role and need for coaching.

* **God coached Cain** (Gen. 4:6–16). Cain's choices after the coaching session did not go well (he killed his brother Abel), but God spoke truth and gave helpful direction.

* **God coached Joshua** (Josh. 1). Joshua found himself in a tough leadership situation (he was replacing a legend, Moses, as leader). God gave clear, motivational, and inspiring advice to this new leader. Joshua's choices are indication he responded favorably to God's coaching session.

* **The prophets coached Israel and Judah** (pick a prophet). Each prophet, speaking for God, gave encouraging, challenging, and difficult coaching to the people. Some took the coaching. Some rejected the coaching. Regardless, God knew his people needed clear direction in response to their "on the field" execution.

* **Jesus coached the Twelve** (pick a Gospel). Jesus had to manage a diverse, sometimes difficult group of apostles (team). He had to redirect their focus and at times create a vision for something they had not imagined from the long-awaited Messiah. Jesus's coaching was at times patient, at times difficult to hear, but always appropriate for the context of the moment. If you consider Jesus's words to the Twelve, other followers, and

religious leaders in Matthew 23, his coaching could be intense and rather harsh.

* **Paul coached Timothy** (1 and 2 Tim.). Paul gave his mentee (Timothy) a lot to think about in his second letter. It's challenging, truth telling, and inspiring. Seriously, if it were captured on video, it would be played regularly in every team meeting. The correspondence has the feel of Lou Gehrig's last speech or a Hall of Fame acceptance speech, a great coaching moment.

There are many more examples (e.g., God's interaction with Moses is a great study). These few are given to demonstrate that *coaching matters*; from the earliest days of humanity, it matters. The examples are also given to demonstrate the various "voices" and "creative styles" in which coaching is executed. There are both soft words and loud words. There are both non-threatening and threatening postures taken. The difference is seen in the situation and context the coach and player find themselves in. We want and desire a coach.

"*The words of coaches will rattle around your head forever.*" I say these words to my athletes at least once a year. Why? Because it is true, and whether positive or negative, I want them to acknowledge the impact a coach can make on their life. My players want to be coached. They want to be coached by someone who knows the game *and* strives to know them apart from the game as well. Again, all of us want and desire a coach.

## HOW?

When you are using God, the prophets, Jesus, and Paul as coaching examples, expectations for finding an athletic coach with such qualities may seem unattainable (read this with a smile and a touch of laughter). Still, if coaching matters, it is important to choose a coach (school, organization, club, etc.) who hits several of the qualities found in such examples. As character and performance coaches, we are often asked by athletes and parents on the style and quality of coaching and programs when deciding where to invest time and resources. How do you decide?

## High-Level Considerations

Every athletic program will have and highlight their superstar, made-it-to-the-next-level alumni. Therefore, when choosing a coach or program, consider the following qualifiers. These are given in no particular order of importance.

* **Reality and rationale.** Does the head coach (competition staff) deal in realities? That is, do they clearly articulate the expectations (practice and play time) for athletes and parents? Coaches who clearly articulate what they expect (practice schedule, before- and after-school trainings, etc.) and their rationale for deciding playing time are giving both the athlete and parent a gift. A gift that helps in deciding whether the "price" will be worth the effort.

* **Records and rumors.** There are no perfect coaches, and we are certainly not asking you to get lost in gossip and negativity (you can find less-than-favorable opinions on all coaches and programs), but it is important to consider the global reputation of these coaches and programs. Often, in our win-at-all-costs culture, winning records can hide poor, even destructive

coaches and coaching styles. Wins and losses do have a part in deciding on a competitive program for an athlete, but they do not give the whole picture. Be careful and listen deeply.

* **Character and culture.** Do the head coach and program have a reputation for character development and building a culture of excellence and winning? Is time given to character and culture development? This can be seen by examining practice schedules (check that time is allotted for character and culture development) but is better "felt" when visiting with coaches. You can sense the difference when character and culture are important.

* **Knowledge and wisdom.** This is a simple but often overlooked consideration when coaches oversell their programs. Does the coach know what they are doing (knowledge), and are they capable of employing various coaching strategies (wisdom)? Both knowledge and wisdom need to be present. Why? A coach who knows the sport (perhaps played at a high level) but only uses yelling and threats when instructing is an unbalanced coach. A coach who can connect and speak to students (has the relational x factor) but has little or no knowledge of the sport they are trying to coach is an unbalanced coach. Balance in both areas is important.

The information for each of these high-level considerations is relatively easy to find by looking on websites (school, conference, district, school, sport specific, etc.), talking to athlete alumni and participants and their parents, visiting with coaches, and touring program facilities.

## Ground-Level Considerations

Let's start by saying that facilities are always a consideration because they demonstrate the support you can expect from school districts and supporting organizations. With that said, you can have excellent facilities and less-than-excellent coaches. What should you consider when looking for a coach? Again, these are not presented by order of importance, do not represent an exhaustive list, and will reflect many of the high-level considerations. Here are qualities you want to look for in a coach.

* **They teach before they yell.** As you saw in the example of Jesus, yelling is a tool in a coach's tool chest. However, it should not be a coach's first move in working with athletes. Today's athletes won't put up with that very long. Parents who believe this is "good coaching" should consider the consequences such coaching styles have on younger athletes who do not have the ability to separate who they are from what they do. It can cause young athletes to lose interest or quit sport and can damage their mental health.[1] With that said, yelling at players, when teaching has been clearly done, is *not* necessarily bad and serves a purpose in the development of an athlete's competitive mindset and character. Note: Yelling at a player does not mean cussing, demeaning, or personalizing comments in a way that connects bad play with being a bad person. Yelling can be particularly useful when coupled with the next quality.

* **They pick up their rocks.** Coaches who call out, punish, yell, or make an example of players and then follow up with the player on why they coached them

the way they did are excellent coaches. They understand that hard coaching must be followed with the same level of positive reinforcement and instruction. Note: Rocks may not be picked up on game day, and this teaching often follows a period in which emotions are lowered and positive communication is achievable.

* **They focus on positives.** A good coach, in our humble opinion, focuses on the positives when coaching away the negatives. This does not mean they are Pollyanna (Google that word if it is new to you; it's perfect here) in their approach. It means they keep the words "can't," "don't," and "hope you can" out of their vocabulary whenever possible. Good coaches know that whatever they speak into the air has the potential to create reality for an athlete.[2]

* **They speak truth.** This goes without saying (especially considering this chapter's introduction). Whether the conversation is about a player's ability, playing time, or athletic future, you want a coach to speak truth to your athlete. Could they be wrong? Sure. Still, good coaches speak the truth they have come to believe based on a player's work, attitude, abilities, team needs, and competitive situation.

* **They accept responsibility.** Good coaches readily accept their mistakes and claim ownership for professional improvement. Most of the coaches we know, of all age and skill levels, work hard to improve their knowledge and wisdom in their specific area of sport. Those who don't accept responsibility and work toward professional improvement do not last long. Note: This is not always true, but be careful of coaches who do

not have the ability to work with other coaches. They often struggle in taking responsibility and blame their mistakes on other coaches or programs. Again, this is not always the case.

* **They coach beyond the field of competition.** This is a particularly important quality for us. At some point, we all must hang up our participation in competitive sport. What then? Coaches who understand the importance of athletics in the development of helpful life habits are priceless. They understand there is life beyond sport. They realize the things they teach, value, say, and do will impact the way their players live their lives after sport. You want a coach who understands this responsibility.

* **They know what they are doing.** Again, this should go without saying, but coaches need to be proficient in their sport. Note: Proficient does not necessarily mean they competed at the highest levels in their sport. There are professional players who have an expert proficiency in their position but lack the qualities of a good coach. The point is simple: you want a coach who knows their craft.

Both the high-level and ground-level considerations contain echoes of the coaching examples found in the Bible. We all want and need quality coaches in our lives—coaches that possess or are committed to growing toward both knowledge and wisdom.

 **NOW?**

If you are reading this book as a parent of a young athlete or are a young athlete yourself, you have some great qualities to look for in your search for a coach and program. If you are a parent of an older athlete or are an older athlete, the situation you face may be a bit different. What do you do now?

* If you are in a healthy situation with a coach and program, be thankful, enjoy, and trust the journey through competitive athletics.
* If you are in an unhealthy situation with a coach and program, use the qualities found in this chapter to have conversations about your concerns with the coach. Hopefully, the coach, your athlete, and you as parent can commit to and forge a healthier future. Also, before you talk with the coach or program coordinator (athletic director or owners), read the chapter "Conflict Matters" for practical guidance.

Remember, there are no perfect coaches, and you will not agree with all decisions, but start with the assumption that your coach has the best of intentions for both your student athlete and team.

"*I remember your dad as a player. He was a great player!*" were the enthusiastic words spoken to my son by the coach who benched me. I had moved back to the Dallas–Fort Worth area to do youth ministry and my old coach, in retirement, became a driver for a local bus company. As blessing would have it, Coach was the driver that night for my youth group activity. We were both surprised when I stepped on his bus. His words were awesome and affirming of my old football memories as a player (cool for my son to hear as well). What followed was a heartfelt thank you to a coach who got to hear how his coaching changed a life. As we recalled the glory days, I was honored to say, "Coach, your words and call to bench me changed my life," and that brought tears to his eyes. I shed a few thankful tears as well.

I ran into the other coach mentioned in the introduction around the same time while attending a funeral for one of my old beloved head coaches. I was standing with a group of friends and teammates when a car pulled up, the window rolled down, and we heard something to the effect of "Hello boys, how are you doing?" We stood speechless. To be honest, that's what we thought he said, we mostly just stood there with our memories drifting back to a time we thought we had forgotten. We hadn't.

A tale of two coaches. One cultivated confidence. One cultivated doubt.

**Coaching matters.**

# CONFLICT
# MATTERS

"Peace is not absence of conflict,
it is the ability to handle conflict by peaceful means."

—Ronald Reagan

"Why is my son being taken off the field?" asked the frustrated, angry, and confused parent.

Full stadium. Full of passion. Full of playoff ramifications. Bright lights. Competitive players. Competitive coaches. The game was decided by a point. A point!

What happened next was unexpected and disappointing. In the "shake the hand" line, a player from the opposing team (the winners) shoved a player, and a conflict-rich environment erupted. The coaches quickly interceded, and the eruption was contained . . . for the most part. The initial "shover" began a victory run across the field, taunting our team. It took a while for his coaches to get him off the field. In the middle of the chaos, a young man was on the brink of engaging with the victory runner. My head coach, wanting to control his players and deescalate the moment, asked for me to remove our player from the field, and I did.

The conduct expected of our players is clearly communicated, but this seemed unfair to the player and his family; they were not happy that their student was unable to join his team on the field while the shover was continuing to taunt players and run around the field.

*I agreed.*

It looked like the situation was about to escalate . . . but the family handled the moment well, and things, while painful, settled.

**Conflict matters.**

## WHY?

You cannot avoid it. Conflict will find you in competitive athletics. As a matter of fact, sport is built around a "conflict" with others and self. Athletes are involved in a contest in which they are trying to win by defeating the other. But you know that is not the type of conflict we are talking about in this chapter. Look at the headlines and you will witness competition (conflict) that has left the field, court, track, or stadium and spilled into parking lots, angry emails, administrative offices, and social media platforms.

Why all the conflict? The Scriptures give us a lot of insight.

> Then the LORD said to Cain, "Why are you angry? Why is your face downcast? If you do what is right, will you not be accepted? But if you do not do what is right, sin is crouching at your door; it desires to have you, but you must rule over it." (Gen. 4:6–7)

> A gentle answer turns away wrath, but a harsh word stirs up anger. (Prov. 15:1)

> A perverse person stirs up conflict, and a gossip separates close friends. (Prov. 16:28)

> They [Paul and Barnabas] had such a sharp disagreement that they parted company. (Acts 15:39)

> Live in harmony with one another. Do not be proud, but be willing to associate with people of low position. Do not be conceited. (Rom. 12:16)

> What causes fights and quarrels among you? . . . You covet but you cannot get what you want, so you quarrel and fight. (James 4:1–2)

This is in the Bible, my friends. Jealousy, anger, gossip, disagreements, arrogance, and coveting are all seen in these passages. Conflict has been a part of humanity for a long time.

Conflict is part of our life. Check out these words from Plato: "I exhort you also to take part in the great combat, which is the combat of life, and greater than every other earthly conflict."[1] The *great combat* is a way to describe the number and nature of conflicts that arise while simply living life with other humans. Now add the stress of competitive athletics. A great combat indeed.

Coaches know conflicts will be faced in the profession. Especially after COVID, the conflicts have escalated.

"Why did that kid get playing time and not mine?"

"That coach has no idea what they are doing and should be fired!"

"I heard that coach was hired because they are friends with the AD!"

"I just can't work with them anymore; they are treating my kid unfairly!"

"I do not want my kid around those type of kids!"

"They are doing things in that program that are just wrong!"

"They don't know how to work with athletes of my kid's talent!"

I have heard and been in the middle of each of these conflict situations (and many that I will not mention here because it would be inappropriate); all are sadly unavoidable but *manageable*. Even though it may take time, discomfort, and pain, everyone involved in a conflict situation can grow and learn from the experience. Sparks may fly, but everyone is sharpened by the process of conflict resolution.

And for the Christ followers reading this book, resolution is what the Father expects from his people.[2] Jesus said to not even think about coming with a gift (acting like all is good because we are going to church) if we have an unresolved problem with another person. It doesn't work that way (Matt. 5:23–24—Fraze paraphrase). John, Jesus's close friend, said that we can't say "I love God" when we hate a brother or sister. People who do this are liars (1 John 4:19–21—Fraze paraphrase). Because I know myself and what is in my heart when in conflict, I keep the above words of John close to my heart in difficult situations with other coaches, parents, and athletes.

You may be thinking, *my athletic experience is not among "brothers and sisters," so these expectations do not apply.* To this I respond, Do you remember Jesus's somewhat confusing words in the Sermon on the Mount? "Be perfect, therefore, as your heavenly Father is perfect" (Matt. 5:48). Go back and look at the context. These words were spoken at the end of several difficult relationship teachings, and specifically in the context of loving our enemies. Enemies! The Father's perfect love is witnessed in sacrifice. He expects the same from us. It matters how we handle conflict.

## HOW?

Conflicts can and should be managed to a productive conclusion. In my opinion, there are two things that are basic to learning how to manage conflict. First, those involved in a conflict need to believe in, commit to, and want to work toward a resolution. These are good words for coaches, parents, and athletes to remember in today's high-stakes athletic environment. Second, those involved in conflict should approach such moments with a commitment to certain nonnegotiable first-step actions. Other actions will be suggested below, but starting every conflict with the following two actions will lead to better, more productive outcomes.

One, listen before you speak (get the story right first). It slows down the escalation of anger. And two, check your attitude and actions (approach conflict with humility). It may not be obvious, but there are always two sides in a disagreement.[3] This is a great starting point for all of us facing a conflict situation. For the sake of confidentiality, we cannot go into detail, but Dr. Williams and I have been involved in many (not an exaggeration) sport-related conflicts that could have been avoided or resolved quickly if all the information was fully known and those involved came into the situation with humility. When emotions run hot, and they will, it benefits us to remember these two basic things before engaging.

"It is not a matter of if but when" is a familiar phrase to most readers. Conflicts can be difficult, and in sport, get ready, they *always feel personal*. With that in mind, even if a specific "problem" is not present, systemic advice for handling interpersonal conflict is helpful in navigating any conflict scenario.[4]

It is possible you are reading this chapter because you are in the middle of a conflict with your coach right now. If so, this is not an exhaustive list, but we have a few suggestions for minimizing and working through conflict.

## Follow the Process

If the coach or program has clearly communicated the process for dealing with conflict, follow the process. It has been our experience that most, if not all, coaches and programs clearly communicate the process for managing conflict. Here are some of the most common elements found in competitive athletic programs:

* **Twenty-four hour rule.** Coaches know the importance of and typically demand a twenty-four-hour cooling off period after a competition to discuss your concerns. This is a great practice because it gives both coach and family time to gather facts and lower emotions.
* **Playing time.** Coaches typically do not want to talk to parents about this subject. With that said, if they do engage parents, they will ask for the athlete to be present for the conversation.
* **Discipline.** Coaches, while preferring the athlete be present, will still speak with parents about the discipline of *their* student. Coaches will not speak about the discipline given to other students.
* **Fan behavior.** This has become more of an issue with the increase in aggressive, even violent, behavior from parents and other fan participants. Any verbally abusive personal threat or demeaning comments can lead to warnings, penalties, removal, and bans from competitive venues.

* **General complaint.** Parents and athletes could have complaints about several things in the athletic experience. Typically, a process for handling conflict scenarios is clearly communicated in a parent/athlete meeting. In short, follow the process.
* **Meetings.** Coaches have preseason (sometimes in-season) meetings to go over expectations and procedures. Go to these! Many a conflict can be defused or managed to satisfaction if the expectations outlined at such meeting are followed.
* **Mediation.** Your conflict may not be solved by talking to the coach. If so, it is possible to visit with their supervisor (head coach or athletic director). That is appropriate when you feel your concern has not been adequately handled. Note: Move up, not down, the chain of command. That is, parents who run straight to the head coach or athletic director (and in some cases principles, school board members, and superintendents) are only escalating the conflict and making it worse for their student athlete.

## Wise Conflict-Management Principles

If the coach or program has not clearly communicated the process for dealing with conflict, your next moves will be more difficult; still, follow wise practices for handling conflict. Several of the practical suggestions below originated from the list of resources given in the notes and Scripture. I have used all these in my years as coach and as a parent of an athlete.

* **Be the adult.** Conflict scenarios have the potential to bring out the worst in everybody. Our athletes are watching our lead and will develop into the humans

we are modeling for them. Often, the way we handle the conflict is more impactful to our athletes than the reason we fight in the first place. Be the adult even if coaches, athletes, parents, and others are not acting appropriately.

* **Set the environment.** If a conflict erupts during or on the way to an event (in a bus, locker room, etc.), coaches have no choice but to secure the environment and get the conflicting parties away from the group to process the situation and reset team focus. If possible, a trusted adult (typically another coach) will be witness to the conflict management process. Whenever possible, ask to meet with your athlete's coach in their office to discuss the conflict situation. As stated above, having your athlete with you is important and lets the coach know you are interested in a solution.

* **Pray.** Always give your time to the Lord. As Matthew 18:20 tells us, Jesus joins us in conflict mediation.[5]

* **Remain calm.** This is your leverage and strength in conflict. Even if you are being yelled at, remain calm. Your calmness will lower the tension and give the best opportunity for your words to be heard. Without control, everyone will be on the offensive in being defensive.

* **Listen before you speak.** When challenged, it is natural to stop listening and begin formulating a response. Fight this natural urge. It is possible you will hear another side of the story than the one communicated to you by your athlete (this happens often).

* **Be aware of triangulation.** When out of balance, it is human to reach out for something that can restore balance (e.g., you are falling and throw out an arm to

catch yourself). Conflict creates unbalance, and most reach out to another person in an attempt to restore balance. Hopefully, such a reach will result in wise counsel (a family member, friend, or leader). However, it can result in unhealthy partnerships with unwise and toxic people who have nothing to do with the conflict, love being in the middle, and have already developed a poor opinion of the coach. Being aware of who or what is being angled for balance will help you understand the real origin of and players in the conflict.[6]

* **Talk to, not around, the issue.** Do not beat around the bush. It may be uncomfortable, but speak directly to the issue(s) you have with the coach or program. For instance, if you are about to tell a coach that their language and tone toward your athlete was out of line, tell them exactly what you know. You need not be rude or disrespectful, but you need to be direct for clarity and then listen for a response.

* **Talk to, not around, those involved.** Recalling the need for "triangle" awareness, be sure you are meeting with those directly involved in the conflict. You may have to make a judgment call based on the severity of the conflict, but typically, the best conflict work happens when meeting with those directly involved in the situation. Seriously, saying things like "Several have told me" to bolster your argument is only creating more tension and division, and the *several* are only a few disgruntled people. The people directly involved should do the visiting.

* **Work toward resolution.** If possible, find a collaborative solution (win-win) to the conflict. This type

of resolution comes from all parties accepting their responsibility in the conflict and resulting solution. A compromised solution (win-lose) takes the same type of responsibility, but involves one or both parties conceding something. If a resolution is not possible, a withdrawal of conflict should be agreed upon until another meeting can be arranged or a higher "mediating" level meeting agreed upon.[7]

* **Restate the resolution and next steps.** If one has been reached, summarize the resolution and each party's responsibility (next steps) to assure that resolution is followed.

* **Take and keep notes.** Shortly after the meeting, record the who, what, when, where, and how of the conflict. Keep those notes in a secure file location. This will provide a valuable resource if a conflict flares up or expands to legal action.

* **Know your conflict style.** Coaches, parents, and players do not get to use, nor should they use, the "I just get angry easily" or "I don't like to talk" to avoid a conflict situation. It is useful for coach, parent, and player to know how they conduct themselves in a conflict situation. Do you avoid conflict? Do you go into combat mode when challenged? You can find your style by taking an online inventory.[8] By the way, pay particular attention to your second-highest conflict style. We turn to our second when unable to use the first.

The coach knows you are angry and is waiting for you in their office. Your athlete is asking to quit the sport they love because of their coach. A fistfight broke out in the middle of the locker room and your athlete has a broken nose. You are not alone. No coach, parent, or athlete enjoys the burden of an upcoming conflict. Take a deep breath, pray, and step into the conflict.

## Select and Interscholastic Coaches

A short but important bit of information concerning conflicts between select coaches and interscholastic coaches: Athletes and parents, especially those of elite skill, should know they will hear conflicting messages on skill level, playing time, practice schedules, strength and conditioning, and more. Our opinion and experience would say to be careful and discerning of those who can make money off your athlete's involvement.[9]

 **NOW?**

Again, you may be reading this chapter first because you are in the middle of a conflict. What now? Commit to handle the situation, no matter how emotionally charged, with a collaborative and mutually beneficial resolution. I know, easier said than done.

* If the coach or program has clearly communicated the conflict resolution process, follow the process to the finish.
* If no clear process exists, follow the suggestions given that best suit your context and work toward resolution.

One final practical suggestion. Yes, I know there are exceptions (the coaching/athletic community typically takes care of these types of individuals and programs),[10] but give your coach the benefit of the doubt. They truly love their job, athletes, and sport.

The player escorted off the field was awarded All-District, instrumental in our team's first district championship and play-off win in close to a decade. His family, there for the entire ride, demonstrated to their son that he was supported, valued, and worth fighting for and modeled how conflict scenarios can be navigated with directness and class and can result in a positive outcome.

**Conflict matters.**

# FAILURE
# MATTERS

"I can accept failure, everyone fails at something.
But I can't accept not trying."

—Michael Jordan

**"The kid took the trophy that my kid just won and ran crying,** hiding behind his mom!" reported my academic dean and friend, the parent of a highly successful high school age nationally ranked tennis player.

"He took the trophy and did what?" was my response. I had to verify the unbelievable story he just told me.

The second telling verified the first; this ugly scene indeed took place, and—there's more—the mom was defending the kid and excusing his immature response to losing a match.

I truly wish this was an isolated incident. However, such scenes play out more often than we want to admit and, unfortunately, can play themselves out through physical altercation.

Do you want to develop a truly competitive athlete? Teach them how to handle and learn from failure.

**Failure matters.**

**WHY?**

Failure happens. It not only happens; it is a vital element in personal, emotional, spiritual, and competitive growth. Vital![1] Consider the process of a baby's first steps. It is a rather awkward, one-step, glorious *fail*. Regardless, a phone captures the moment in video, shared with grandparents and friends, with the caption "baby's first steps." The *failure* is seen and understood as a step toward walking. Again, failure, if handled correctly, is the catalyst for success.[2] There are several famous "fails" and corresponding growth opportunities in the Bible.

The Bible is filled with failure. Read that last sentence again; I will wait. Failure is not to be "celebrated" or "accepted" without challenge (Rom. 6), but it is to be expected as a normal part of personal, spiritual, and professional growth. Failure is found in our most beloved and elevated heroes of the Bible:

**Adam and Eve**. Well, you know about their choice in trees.

**Abraham**. He had some trouble relying on his own armed force, lying and reproducing.

**Sarah**. She laughed and gave her servant to her husband.

**Joseph**. He may have been a bit too proud of his dream-interpreting abilities.

**Moses**. He murdered an Egyptian guard. Oh, and the whole placing-himself-in-the-position-of-God thing with the water-out-of-the-rock episode?

**Samson**. He gave up his gift of strength because he had a habit of not saying no to beautiful women.

**Lot's wife**. A reminder to not get salty.

**David**. Where do we start? Adultery, murder, dishonesty, pride, revenge, and more are on his list of failures.

**Peter**. Well, he cut a guy's ear off and denied Jesus. And . . . he struggled with racism.

**Paul**. He took Christians into custody and presided over the execution of Stephen.

You may have been uncomfortable and had to fact check some of those. Why? For most of us, we concentrate on the highlight reels of biblical heroes (Heb. 11) and downplay or ignore the blooper reels that make them the great examples of faith they truly are. Fact: for every failure listed above, you can see how God used these moments to refine, discipline, and grow each of these giants of faith. In short, *failure is not fatal*. However, read carefully, because failures do have teachable moments—consequences:

**Adam and Eve**. They had to live outside the Garden.

**Abraham**. He had trouble with Lot and Ishmael.

**Sarah**. She developed and fought a bad case of jealousy.

**Joseph**. He ended up in a pit.

**Moses**. He spent forty years in the desert.

**Lot's wife**. She became a pillar of salt.

**Samson**. He lost his eyesight and then his life.

**David**. He lost his son(s) and his kingdom (though he found it again) and brought death on Israel.

**Peter**. He was in a dark place for a while.

**Paul**. He was feared and misunderstood.

As you can see, not all consequences are the same, because not all failures are the same. However, there are consequences. Here is the great news, though: God does not waste the pain of failure. Take some time to read Hebrews 12:4–12. Yes, the topic of conversation is the discipline of hardships, but the actions of God, as seen in the lives of the heroes above, are normative. If we allow him to (another topic for another time), God will use our failure as an opportunity to help us grow and learn.[3]

In the same way, the pain of life (often caused by our own or someone else's failure) is never wasted. Take a moment and read this verse, slowly: "Not only so, but we also glory in our sufferings, because we know that suffering produces perseverance; perseverance, character; and character, hope" (Rom. 5:3–4). Do you see the progression through and use of suffering? The progression of *perseverance, character, hope* works in life and, wait for it, competitive athletics.

For our purpose here, it is rather easy to see in the biblical narrative how failure was, and still can be, used as a catalyst for change and character building. So if you are in the midst of a learning period produced by failure, "Strengthen your feeble arms and weak knees" (Heb. 12:12). In other words, stop feeling sorry for yourself, learn your lesson, and improve your performance.

Parents, if you never let your kid fall while learning to walk, you would still be carrying them. It is painful to watch your student athlete fail, but let them. If not, you will be carrying them and will damage their ability to develop as a higher-performing athlete and, more importantly, a person. Failure is a catalyst.

I have been part of the rebuilding process with three football programs. Each of these programs, led by outstanding head coaches, used failure as a catalyst of growth. When success eventually came, it was typically witnessed in a dramatic, awesome moment of victory.

> Going 1–9 for two consecutive years and winning the state championship a few years later started with a dramatic, tough win in the last game of the season.

> Overcoming two fourteen-point deficits to win the first playoff game in over twenty years started with a win over a top-rated powerhouse district rival.

> Going from 0–10 in the first year to district champions in five years started with a multiple-overtime win against a tough crosstown rival.

A special moment that validated the long, patient process through failure into victory. A moment that signaled we will no longer be everyone's homecoming game team selection. It all started with getting comfortable with failure.

# HOW?

Here is the great takeaway for parents: *let your student athlete fail*. And here is the great takeaway for student athletes: *failure is not fatal and is a catalyst for growth*. I am certain both points have become apparent by this point in the chapter. However, if it was so easy to do, we would not have written this chapter. How do we embrace failure? The answer is different for both parent and student athlete.

## Tips for Parents

Let's start with suggestions for how parents can embrace failure.

***Change your mindset toward failure.*** Your kid will not succeed in everything they do. They will fail. Failure is a gift. The failure of your kid is not ˈ*necessarily* a reflection of your failure as a parent (read that last sentence again and check the endnote).[4] It is difficult work, but change your mindset and then help your student athlete with their mindset toward failure. Failure is a catalyst!

How does one change their mindset? We can start with how you talk about the failure episode. *First*, listen to your athlete. Just listen and let them vent. If they don't want to talk about the failure, give it time and let the emotions settle. *Second*, don't offer excuses, thereby negating your student athlete's part in the failure (e.g., "If they had caught your passes, you would have had a great game," or "If the coach had called the right play, you would have won the game"). There could be a degree of truth in both statements; however, no good is done by deflecting blame. *Third*, focus the failure moment on the created (and often obvious) catalyst moment (e.g., "I am so sorry about this loss; what did you learn from the experience?"). Of course, such questions come after the emotions have settled. Your first step in changing your mindset is changing the way you talk about the failure. This will relate to the next suggestion; how you talk about failure moments in the stands says a lot about your mindset (and character).

***Manage your own emotional reaction to failure.*** As a coach, I can get pretty fired up in a failure moment. As a parent, if you witness my emotional reaction in the stands, you may not even think I am paying attention. Why? I am managing my emotional reaction to failure. What's the difference between parent and coach? As a coach, I am immediately connected to the moment, and a response to the failure episode is part of the catalyst opportunity. As a parent, I am not on the field or directly impacting the competition. I still have emotion but manage the emotion differently.

Note that as both parents and coaches, the authors of this book strive to be respectful, articulate, and appropriate in our response to competition failures. Here are two emotional-management suggestions. *First*, give yourself a time-out (breathe, take a walk around the court or field, remove yourself from toxic fans and situations, etc.). Time-outs do wonders in controlling your level of emotion. *A word of caution*: the higher your student athlete rises in competition and prominence, the greater amount of verbal and written criticism they will receive from the stands, social media, strangers, and friends. Get yourself prepared and manage your emotions. *Second*, most coaches have a twenty-four-hour response-time rule. Create that time for yourself. Don't talk about the failure moment with your student athlete or coach (we will talk about that below) until a twenty-four-hour period has passed. I have witnessed, more than once, a parent's overreaction to their athlete's tears or anger with a failure episode involving a coach, other player, or other team. Calm down and get the facts straight before blowing things up in your anger. Manage your emotional reaction to failure.

***Trust the process.*** This phrase is used a great deal between coaches and athletes. It is a simple way to remember, even in failure, that we have a plan for handling it and using it as a catalyst for getting better. Again, having the ability to fail and then learn from that failure is a critical part of athletic and personal growth. As a parent, it may be painful to watch (e.g., if your kid is benched, a voice is raised, etc.), but *trust the process* when your student athlete experiences a failure moment.

## Tips for Athletes

Understanding that the above suggestions for handling failure can be helpful for athletes as well as parents, let's continue with a couple of suggestion on how student athletes can better embrace and use failure.

***Ask the hard questions of yourself.*** It is easy to blame others for your failures. And in some cases, another's actions can create failure for you. Even so, as the athlete, ask yourself hard reflection questions to turn failure into an opportunity for growth:

* What could I have done better in this situation?
* What was my practice like the week before the game?
* How did I prepare mentally for the competition?
* How did I prepare physically for the game?
* Is there anything I could have done differently to avoid this failure? If so, why didn't I do it during the game?
* In what ways am I not taking responsibility for this failure? How am I taking too much responsibility?

* Am I able to move beyond this failure moment? Why or why not?
* Was the failure caused by my lack of emotional, mental, or physical toughness?
* Was I coachable during the failure episode? How did I react? Did I move on to the next play or lose it with myself, my team, and my coaches?

These types of questions are helpful to reflect on during and after a failure and will lead you into growth opportunities. Note: If you are one who "loses it" when a failure moment occurs, work on that quickly. It hurts your team, your leadership, and the opportunity you may have to play at the next level (pay attention to the conclusion of this chapter).

***Work on the thing(s) that led to failure.*** There will be a moment in which the thing(s) that led up to the moment of failure are identified, sometimes painfully identified (e.g., "the film doesn't lie"). Decide to work on those things. It really is that simple. However, if you blame others or shift blame (there is typically a lot of blame to go around for both coach and players), you will create unneeded tension in and for yourself, the team, and your family. Take responsibility for your part and work on the thing(s) that led to the failure. Remember, failure is not fatal; it is an opportunity for change. Failure is part of the process; get comfortable with it.

***Don't accept failure.*** It is possible that you, and your parent, got the idea that failure should be accepted without struggle. That is not our message at all. *It should be understood as an unavoidable part of personal and athletic growth, but never accepted.* Have the strength to identify areas of growth and the grit to do something about those areas so failure can be replaced with personal and team improvement and victories.

## When to Get Involved

There is an elephant in the room when it comes to failure and your student athlete. As a parent, when should you step in and address your athlete's failure with a coach? Here are a few things to consider before jumping into your athlete's failure moment(s):

***When emotional or physical harm is present.*** This does not mean an episode of hurt feelings, tears, or sadness. That happens when coaching occurs. What we are addressing here is a pattern of emotional or physical harm that is obvious, ongoing, and witnessed. The coaching profession, and many organizations, do a great job of policing the conduct of coaches and staff. However, especially in our win-at-all-costs environment, some coaches are allowed to "do what it takes" to win. You are the parent and should always have your student's emotional and physical health as priority. Therefore, if you feel harm is occurring, set up a meeting with your coach first and then take the matter to a higher authority if needed (read "Conflict Matters"). Note: Student athletes can exaggerate or even lie to their parents in the face of hard coaching or failure moments. So get the facts straight before destroying a coach's career. Often, there is more to the story than you are hearing.

***When your student athlete has attempted and is unable to handle the failure situation alone.*** Before intervening, especially with older athletes, coach your student on how they should talk to and personally address their failure moment with their coach. After the initial conversation, if the matter is not progressing toward repair, take your student with you and address the failure moment with the coach together (read "Conflict Matters").

## NOW?

Parents, *let your student athlete fail.* Commit to changing your mindset toward failure and encourage grit in your student athlete by letting them grow from failure experiences. If you continue to move leagues, coaches, organizations, and schools when failure occurs so your student can have "success," it is time you realize the issue may be with your student's actual playing ability and not the place or coach.

Athletes, *failure is not fatal and is a catalyst for growth.* No one is perfect. Get comfortable with failure, but never accept it as the only possible outcome. Commit to being honest in failure moments, being coachable, and trusting the process of growth it offers.

Finally, consider that failure can serve as a mirror that helps determine your future in competitive athletics. Few play their competitive sport(s) in middle school, fewer in high school, fewer yet in college (all levels), and very few at the professional level. At some point, your athletic career will end. That can be a painful experience. Your failure to compete and play may be a gift. Discern carefully.

Trent Grisham is a Golden Glove outfielder with the San Diego Padres. In high school, Trent was the top Major League Baseball prospect in the Dallas–Fort Worth area and would later be the first-round pick (fifteenth overall) in the 2015 MLB draft by the Milwaukee Brewers. Each of his games (and many practices) brought dozens of MLB scouts, players, and managers to the field. On one occasion while playing in a competitive district game, Trent struck out. What happened next was interesting.

The general manager for one MLB team was in the crowd and personally wanted to watch Grisham play to assess his professional ability. (Fun fact, there were over one hundred scouts at our baseball field that day.) Trent played well, very well actually, but the manager wanted to see what happened when Grisham failed. So when he struck out (which did not happen often), the general manager watched Trent walk to the dugout. He kept watching his reaction to . . . here it comes . . . *failure*. As always, Trent did not throw his bat or yell at others or any of several other things he could have done to handle his disappointment. He simply walked back, learned from his failure at bat, shared his wisdom with his teammates, and then dominated the next at bat.

**Failure matters.**

# FUN MATTERS

"At the end of the day, if I can say I had fun,
it was a good day."

—Simone Biles

A few years ago, I (Monica) asked our daughter Soraya, "Why do you like to run?"

She thought for a minute and then calmly said, "Mommy, I feel free."

During a session with a competitive athlete, I asked this individual who was struggling in their sport when they last enjoyed playing. The individual said it was when they were three or four years old. I asked why, and the athlete answered, "Because it was fun!" Each chapter in this book culminates in a challenge to keep sport fun.

**Fun matters.**

 ## WHY?

Competitive sport speaks to an end to winning. Winning may come at the cost of fun in sport, which diverges from its original intent, to play. The current sports model provides space for competitive athletes to display talents and skills developed through an extensive commitment to training.

The high-impact, high-stakes environment in competitive settings follows an excessive training and practice model that compromises the exploration and selection of other identity-forming activities. Researchers have criticized the benefits of competitive sport, saying it negatively impacts participants' health and emotional well-being. This is true only when athletes align their identity with what they do, parents forget to be fans, coaches forget athletes are people and not machines, and fun is de-emphasized.[1]

## Progression of Sport from Play to Work

*Play.* "I *play* basketball." "Did you see that *play*?" Play is a "free activity involving exploration, self-expression, dreaming, and pretending; it follows no firm rules and can take place anywhere."[2] The progression from *play* to *work* in sports arrests the purest form of *play* in exchange for competition. One of the unintended consequences of diluting *play* in sports is that athletes are conditioned to lean on a socially oriented sense of *perfectionism*.

*Perfectionism.* Perfectionism is socially engineered social comparisons and evaluations. Parents, coaches, and elite athletes define excellence. They also determine the process for evaluating and attaining excellence. This socially prescribed perfectionism may cause athletes to acquiesce their identity to a set of publicly stipulated standards. Young athletes learn to perform, portray, and conform to fit the competitive sport model versus establishing what process and achievement look like similar to how our kids play.

Again, sport in and of itself is benign and can teach participants valuable life lessons. The criticisms leveled against competitive sports concern the de-emphasis on fun where the athletes matter. Historically, this was the case.

***History of Modern Sport.*** In 1869, Harvard and Oxford Universities' boat club participants challenged each other to a boat contest from Putney to Mortlake in London, and Oxford's team beat Harvard's. Though the contest was a fun-spirited, simple event that involved a culturally popular sport, the contest morphed to a competitive, higher-stakes model.

The contest between Harvard and Oxford spurred other rowing challenges. Student and administrator involvement in the contests added more significance and increased performance demands. The challenge became less participant-centric and more outcome-focused and competitive.

The Harvard–Oxford example mirrors present-day youth sport models. Young athletes are recruited into sports under the guise of fun with friends. Quickly, fun is omitted, and friend groups are subject to a weeding-out process. This is unfortunate given the importance of social environment on child development in play and relationships.[3]

Asking parents, coaches, and athletes to protect fun in competitive athletics has biblical precedence. "You who are young, be happy while you are young, and let your heart give you joy in the days of your youth" (Eccles. 11:9). Sounds like the fun kids have when they play, right?

Have you ever watched kids play? They often make up the rules as they go. Rules emerge as individuals mature. There is flexibility, and identity is not connected to the outcome. All kids are welcome to participate in the game. Consequently, participation in youth sports makes the process of moving beyond a competition narrative into a space of self-discovery much more tenuous by divorcing sports play from its original intent to play.

Solomon, outside of Christ, is the wisest man to have lived. Dr. Fraze and I find it interesting that he would add a note on fun. Ecclesiastes tells young folks to enjoy what they do. Have fun. They can only do so if adults make fun a priority.[4]

## HOW?

Ironically, it takes work to delete fun from sport, because fun with friends is the reason kids start playing. Play is inherent in sport when sport is done right. Here are a few practical ways to keep sport fun.

- **Let athletes help define what their relationship with sport looks like.** In other words, do they want to be involved casually or do they plan other activities around sport involvement?
- **Let the kids play.** For instance, Marcus and I coached our son's basketball team. During one game, I looked over and saw two of the players belly-down on the court pretending to swim in the middle of the game. I smiled at the boys and said, "Wrong sport!" The boys stood up and I asked, "Are you guys ready now? If so, hustle and guard someone."
- **Celebrate non-athletic accomplishments.** Parents, celebrate them as enthusiastically as athletic wins.
- **Parents and coaches, remain fans** of the athletes and the sports you are involved with.
- **Highlight them winning.** For example, point out an athlete doing a drill or skill right to direct the attention

of other athletes to that behavior. You achieve two
goals: you encourage the one doing it right, and you
provide the model for what you want rather than criti-
cizing the one who is getting it wrong. Try this method
a few times; you will be surprised how well it works.[5]

* **Listen.** I am reminded that Paul told Timothy, "Don't
let anyone look down on you because you are young,
but set an example for the believers in speech, in
conduct, in love, in faith and in purity" (1 Tim. 4:12).
Involve the athletes in the conversation about their
performance (see the chapter "Parenting Matters"
for pregame, postgame, and practice prompts for
your athlete).

* **Keep practices light but focused.** Let the athletes
know what you want to achieve in practice, and give
them their collective and individual roles.

* **Compete.** You can make anything in sport a "competition." Yes, having winners and losers is not a bad thing,
leads to a number of life lessons, and can drive fun.
Even losses can be leveraged to increase desire and
sport competency. It should be fun to compete.

This is not an exhaustive list of ways to keep fun in sport, but it
is a good start. These practical tips pertain to keeping sport fun
for athletes, but coaches want to have fun in sport, too.

A few years ago, I watched a documentary on John Wooden.
Wooden won several NCAA Division I men's basketball
national championships. Coach Wooden was known for recit-
ing a seven-point creed for life and the "Two Sets of Three" he
learned from his father. The seven points were: be true to yourself; make each day your masterpiece; help others; drink deeply

from good books, especially the Bible; make friendship a fine art; build a shelter against a rainy day; and pray for guidance and give thanks for your blessings every day.[6]

The Two Sets of Three were just as simple. Set one: never lie, never cheat, and never steal. Set two: don't whine, don't complain, and don't make excuses. Simple truths handed down from his father and revealed in the Bible shaped Wooden's life and steered the way he loved his wife, fathered his children, and coached basketball.

Coach Wooden chose to commit to the whole person of each player and gave the athlete permission to bring his whole self to the table. The result was that the UCLA Bruins men's basketball team was successful. Coach Wooden's approach to coaching, and especially his relationship with his players, is radical in today's sports structure where the pursuit of winning takes precedence over relationships.

Wooden shows adults and coaches that godly principles and sincere relationships with athletes do not have to be compromised to be successful. At the heart of Wooden's work is a balanced approach to life that results in enjoyment and appreciation for the sport and its players. That balance resulted in *fun*.

One day, Soraya was running and jumping in the backyard, playing with the leaves on a low-hanging branch. Soraya ran, jumped, and swiped at the leaves at least a half-dozen times until she decided to move on to another activity. There was no attachment to the activity, no evaluation, and no conclusions drawn that would denote achievement or failure.

For Soraya, failing to grab the leaves did not make her a failure any more than grabbing the leaves would make her a winner. It was play and fun in all its innocence. Soraya set the rules and was at peace regardless of the outcome. Soraya's day in the backyard painted the clearest picture for me of what sport should look like.

**Fun matters.**

# IDENTITY MATTERS

"Had I been a great athlete, I'm not sure I would have even gone into coaching. I may have turned out feeling that my life ended when my athletic career ended, as happens so many times with various athletes."

—Lou Holtz

## "What am I anymore, if I'm not this?"

This is the question Ronda Rousey, former Ultimate Fighting Championship (UFC) bantamweight champion, asked herself after her devastating loss to Holly Holm in a UFC title bout.[1] Rousey's question is one many athletes wrestle with in sports. This question comes in response to a loss, an injury, or any event that challenges the identity the athlete has created or assumed. Many reading this book probably think identity conflicts and struggles only happen at the college or professional levels. The truth is, identity struggles occur in all competitive athletes.

**Identity matters.**

## WHY?

"What do you want to be when you grow up?" is a question all children are asked by adults. It is an early identity question. In Christian families, this question is often answered with a qualifier (e.g., "I want to be a Christian fireman"). Consider Proverbs 23:7 (NKJV), "As he thinks in his heart, so is he." When it comes to identity formation and competitive athletics, thinking can quickly become clouded.

Many involved in sport widely embrace their "athlete" identity roles, effectively "foreclosing other aspects of their identity, e.g., student, club member, volunteer, musician, and artist."[2] The scope of identity investment is equal to the amount of psychological, physical, and emotional energy committed to an athlete's development in their sport. The degree to which the athlete's participation in sport is affirmed by parents, coaches, or teammates reinforces the single-minded investment in the sport identity role.

Sometimes parents introduce confusion or create competition between identities. I have heard Christian parents speak of the importance of Jesus and faith until church camp, Wednesday night services, or Sunday morning fellowship conflicted with practice, game, or tournament schedules. The athlete heard about the importance of faith but experienced Jesus taking a back seat to sport with no mention of Christ en route or before practice or game time. The athlete learned in those moments that the important identity was that of athlete, so they should feed that persona.

## HOW?

Identity is conditioned. In the summer of 1999, someone dear to me took the next step toward a lifelong pursuit of becoming a player in the National Basketball Association (NBA). He had the right contacts, exposure, and evaluators taking notice; he was living up to what *everyone* said he would be. All his life he heard phrases such as, "You're going to *play* in the league!" and even, "You can *play* some ball!" From early on, this individual's participation in sports was marked with opportunities that shaped him in so many ways. He was an athlete. That was who he was and how he thought of himself.

Looking back, it is shocking how much influence competitive sport—select, club, AAU, 3v3, etc.—had on my own identity. For years, I struggled to break free of my identity as an athlete. I was a two-sport college athlete. Why is it that so many athletes struggle with the question, "Who am I?" Ronda Rousey, Brett Favre, Michael Phelps, Naomi Osaka, Misty Copeland, my dear friend, me, and countless others have been snared by the "athlete" identity.[3] Incidentally, all these athletes, me included, started competitive sport "performing" between the ages of four and nine. Young athletes rely on adult perspectives to shape their views of the world and themselves. Many children currently engaged in sports are operating in preset conditions that have an active role in shaping their identity.

Competition is tricky. It can compel athletes to work hard to excel in sport, but it has a dark side. Competition inherently requires social comparison. It is necessary for athletes to compare and measure their performance and approach to sport to someone performing a similar task or position in their sport.[4] In the end, it is about winning. Right?

When winning is the *only* measurement of athletic reward, most of the evaluative messages young athletes receive will be assessments of their sports performance, often void of virtue or character-developing feedback that can promote a healthy identity. Consequently, participation in sports makes the process of moving beyond a competitive narrative into a space of self-discovery much more tenuous by divorcing sports play from its original intent, that is, to *play*. How do we help our student athletes with identity formation in such a world?

## Play

This word prefaces many exchanges between individuals concerning participation in sport or one's role as a spectator. "I *play* basketball" or "Did you see that *play*?" *Play* is the word used by children, parents, and coaches to describe involvement in sport, when in fact, per the definition of *play*, sport in this present age seems misaligned. The word *play* means "free activity involving exploration, self-expression, dreaming, and pretending; it follows no firm rules and can take place anywhere."[5] Sport should emphasize the athlete's desires and experiences over an outcome. We realize that such an athlete-centric model challenges the modern-day take on sports participation, which is set to value the outcome, to win, over participant experience, *to play*. This returns the conversation to the role of sport in promoting the "athlete" identity for all athletes—yes, *all* athletes, not just the elite athletes. Note: Play should and can continue at all levels of competition. However, as your student athlete grows and ages, they will not be guaranteed "playing time" at higher levels of competition (this will be addressed in "Reality Matters").

## Fight Identity Foreclosure

Did I say "foreclosure"? That thing that happens when you have a loan you haven't made regular payments on? If parents and athletes are not diligent, it is very similar. Let's start with a tour of sport history to get a clear look at what we are fighting. To do this, I will condense my dissertation into a few paragraphs (get ready). It is a fight we must win for the health of our student athletes.

The role of sport in sculpting the "athlete" identity began very innocently. The intent of school-based sports circa World War I mirrored intercollegiate sports programs and was adopted to correct fitness levels deemed to be distressingly low. Over time, the regard for school-based sports increased exponentially. This phenomenon is evident in the attendance numbers at high school football games in Texas (e.g., the 2013 Allen v. Pearland game that drew 54,347 fans), also known as the Friday Night Lights phenomenon.[6] This phenomenon directly affects how individuals who participate and excel in sport are perceived by their peers, their school, and their community. Consequently, this level of affirmation will influence how the individual, who likely welcomes the affirmation as an athlete, views him or herself. The adoption of the athlete identity often leads to foreclosing other identities and diverting maximum effort to feeding the athlete persona, which yields a desired result—affirmation—thus leading to a one-dimensional development of interest and ability.

The age athletes start in competitive sport, frankly, matters. As pointed out, most athletes enter into sport "play" between the ages of six and nine years old. This is not an accident; athlete recruitment and development are based on skills-development models that are founded on research applied in the use of long-term athlete development plans, or LTADPs. Using LTADPs deepens the athlete's investment in fueling their athlete persona. Over the years, research has broadened public understanding of development, and sport scientists have tapped these discoveries to tailor athletic training plans to match "critical periods in the life of a young person in which the effects of training can be maximized."[7] The plan spans more than ten years and introduces athletes to sport under the guise of fun with friends; "FUNdamentals" is phase two.

The plans quickly progress athletes into phase two, "Learning to Train," where athletes learn skill development and talent identification, narrow their involvement to three sports, and start mental performance training. Phase three involves training for sport-specific skills development, adding strength training, narrowing sports to two, and including more practices and games. By phase four, the athletes are specialists in one sport and are fully engaged in "Training to Compete."[8]

The LTADP is seemingly innocuous. However, the concept of deliberate practice is at the epicenter of the LTADP framework. Deliberate practice entails goal-oriented, intentional engagement in skills-development activities that move performers from novice to expert executors of the skill(s). This makes the LTADP an invaluable tool in turning sport participants into athletes and, more critically, elite athletes. So, where is the fight? We want our student athletes to be the best they can be at their craft, correct? Yes, but (this is a big *but*) not at the expense of their overall non-athletic identity formation.

 ## NOW?

A few years ago, I researched how elephants are trained in India. When the elephant is very young, a rope is tied around one of its legs and to a stake. The rope used is just strong enough to restrain the young elephant. This process is repeated daily into adulthood, using the same piece of rope. As a result, the elephant is ultimately conditioned to believe the rope and stake can hold it. As one contemplates involvement in sport, sport participation in and of itself does not deserve scrutiny. It is when adults who have a responsibility to young athletes—to love them, protect them, guide them, and allow for the safe and necessary process of self-expression and self-exploration—instead impose their agendas on the athletes that problems ensue. We have tied ropes to stakes. What do we do now?

## Adults Must Examine Their Own Relationship with Sport

How is it that many adults allow their proximity to sport to infringe on their responsibility to promote the process of self-discovery? Maybe sport's role in shaping the adult's sense of self has desensitized them to the potential harm of allowing sports to play such a role in influencing the identity of the young people who have been entrusted to their care. Practically, this it how it looks. Soraya told me she did not want to run "this year because I need to just train and get stronger." An unhealthy relationship with sport would have resulted in a disastrous conversation with Soraya that ended with me forcing her to run to appease my own desire for her to compete.

Until adults recognize the influence of sports in their own lives, they will be hard-pressed to halt the assault of sport on influencing the lives of young people, essentially staking the young person to a flawed view of themselves, a flawed view of their identity, and a flawed view of their involvement in sport.

## Consider the Student Athlete's Experience

Due diligence is given to teaching young athletes the values, norms, antics, attitudes, and discipline to perform in sports and play the game to a degree that appeases the audience (i.e., coaches, parents, and fans). Noticeably absent from the list of those being appeased are the athletes, the performers in sport. Attempts to improve the quality and experience of participation in sports have muted the reasons athletes join sports, such as to have fun and be with friends, replacing play with a rules-based framework focused on a result, and that is, by and large, the nature of work. It invites the question, "Does the athlete's experience even matter?" Self-exploration and healthy identity formation can exist in competitive sport if the sport framework adopts an athlete-centric model. That is up to us. Ultimately, if identity matters, which it does, we must help athletes form healthy relationships with sport, and when it is time, they can put sport down, better for the experiences and grateful for friendships and lessons learned along the way.

Involvement in sport is attractive, and this applies to people in the most densely populated cities or most rural communities. Interestingly, regardless of where sport is played, participation in sport affects identity formation and can result in identity foreclosure. The irony is that athlete identity weakens the athletic experience and compromises play. Athletes play freer and looser when they bring their full selves to the table. In short, they *win more* competitions!

"What am I anymore, if I'm not this?"

These words sound an alarm.

Michael Phelps, Naomi Osaka, Simone Biles, and numerous other athletes have gone public to talk about the toxic world of competitive sports, sharing similar stories of how their identities were so cemented in sport that they did not know who they were apart from that persona. They are telling us we are getting it wrong when athletes can only identify themselves through the sport they play and how well they play it.

**Identity matters.**

# MINDSET
# MATTERS

"Concentrate all your thoughts upon the work in hand.
The sun's rays do not burn until brought to a focus."

—Alexander Graham Bell

**It was a big Friday night in Texas.**

The stands were full to watch the game that would shape the outcome of our district standings and playoff pairings. The offense of the opposing team was heating up and our defense faced a challenging fourth quarter. We needed a couple of stops and the game would be won.

After a particularly rough series of play, one of our young men hobbled off the field. Fatigued, body sore, and bearing the strain of smashmouth and trench-battle football, his body language communicated he was finished. We did not need him to show that mindset to himself, his team, and the opposing sidelines.

I pulled the player close, looked him in the eye, and asked, "Are you hurt or hurting?"

To be clear, if a player is hurt, they are injured and quickly assessed by professionals and attended to. A player's health is more important than a win. But if a player's mindset shifts, coaches attend to that as well. If not attended to, a player's mindset can create doubt in others and team energy can spiral down.

"Are you hurt or hurting?" was a valid question and one that needed to be answered quickly.

**Mindset matters.**

## WHY?

Time for a simple, concise definition of what we mean by *mindset*. Mindset is that which a person consistently thinks about themselves, their ability to handle various stimuli, and their attitude in responding.[1] There are various types of mindsets addressed in research. For our purposes, the one you will see highlighted and assumed in this chapter is a *growth mindset*. This type of mindset is popular in both academic and athletic worlds for obvious reasons. Those with a growth mindset seek and demand improvement in their performance.

There is a connection between what we think (mindset) and what we do. The connection has been researched, resourced, and codified for use by performance coaches and therapists for years.[2] Mindset matters in relationship to an athlete's performance, and it matters in the way we live life. Why? We were created with this brain–body connection.

Genesis chapters 1 and 2 indicate humanity was created in the "image of God," possesses the "breathe of life," and was given responsibility "to rule over" creation and live as "one flesh" with each other. There are many mindset ramifications packed in all four of these quotations. In my opinion, the greatest mindset demonstration is seen in the central, foundational, passionate call to the community of Israel's obedience: "Love the Lord your God with all your *heart* and with all your *soul* and with all your *strength*" (Deut. 6:5—emphasis mine). Did you see it? The mindset, thinking and devotion (heart and soul), translates into practical, physical action (strength). A good mindset results in good action; the opposite is also true because the two are connected.

Another of my favorite examples of the power of a good mindset is seen in Paul's words to the Philippians. For context, Paul is in prison. From his cell, Paul provides a message of encouragement, outlining a pathway in which joy is found in difficult circumstances. The letter contains the famous "I can do all things through Christ who strengthens me" statement (4:13 NKJV). A statement that is often taken out of context by athletes, the words demonstrate Paul's confidence in his ability to survive and thrive in all of life's imaginable circumstances. How has this confidence developed? His mindset translated into action. You can see this relationship in the message he gives *before* the "I can do all things" statement: "Whatever is true, whatever is noble, whatever is right, whatever is pure, whatever is lovely, whatever is admirable—if anything is excellent or praiseworthy—*think about such things*" (Phil. 4:8—emphasis mine).

There is a lot of mindset material in this section of Scripture. The emphasized words are where I want you to focus your attention. Do you see it? One's negative physical circumstances can be transformed and endured through focusing on that which is good. Mindset matters to the way we live life and compete as athletes.

## HOW?

I ask athletes, "Why did the *Titanic* sink?" They typically respond with, "It hit an iceberg." I follow up with, "Hitting the iceberg caused the initial problem. The *Titanic* sunk because the collision caused damage to the watertight compartments." Without use of those compartment doors, the spreading flood was unavoidable and ended tragically. Many factors demonstrate an arrogance from operators that the "unsinkable ship" was immune from fatal failure. However, only four days into the maiden voyage, the *Titanic* lay two miles down on the Atlantic Ocean floor.[3] Why the *Titanic*?

There are many similarities between the sinking of this great ship and the sinking of an athlete's mindset in competition. Those who made and sailed the *Titanic*, because of the impressive physical features of the ship, appeared to be arrogant and above sound sailing practices. Today, we would call this a *fixed mindset*. That is, what you believe is set and unchangeable. Well, we know how it worked out for those in charge of the *Titanic*. If not intentionally addressed, especially in the life of elite athletes, the physical assets create an arrogant and often difficult-to-coach athlete. This can cause a tragic sinking event for the student athlete.

As discussed above, the mental and physical self are related in such a way that one influences the level of performance of the other. Beginning with the truth that mindset matters, the following are a few of my favorite coaching strategies for supporting the development of a growth mindset.

## Identity–Actions–Feelings

My basic coaching strategy for mindset development begins with identity (read "Identity Matters" for more on this foundational element in an athlete's mindset development and corresponding performance). We must first understand and teach that human identity should be grounded in who we are aside from what we do. I continue with the athletic identity that one accepts when they decide to participate in a chosen sport or team. That identity leads to a set of *actions* that are expected to be executed, even when they don't feel like it, with the highest effort and attitude.

A word on these two execution terms, "effort" and "attitude." These are the two non-coachable qualities an athlete brings to their sport. Coaches can discipline a lack of both, but the execution of each are the sole responsibility of the athlete. The *feelings* experienced after the completion of a great training, practice, or game come after, and because of, an accepted *identity* that corresponded with a set of accomplished *actions*. *Identity* leads to *actions* lead to *feelings*. The progression is crucial to the development of a vibrant growth mindset. If reversed, an unhealthy fixed mindset is developed.

Athletes whose starting point is their feelings often don't *feel* like . . .

> . . . getting to practice on time.
> . . . going to practice.
> . . . giving maximum effort.
> . . . listening to the coach's direction.
> . . . following team rules.
> . . . passing their classes.

The *actions* of such athletes are unreliable. Such athletes sink their personal athletic careers or create an iceberg collision that floods the team ship with negativity. As a coach, I find it humorous when such athletes are cut or have their playing time limited and then fight to claim an *identity* that was never earned.

## Stay Positive

This is probably the most "practical" of practical suggestions for maintaining a healthy mindset. Every athletic journey has its negative moments and opportunities to develop a negative mindset (injury, failure, transition, coaching changes, team dynamics, negative coaching experiences, etc.). Negativity can destroy an athlete's future and destroy team dynamics. Even in such challenging moments, an athlete (and parents) can decide to possess and maintain a mindset that is positive. Positivity helps the athlete find the lesson(s) gained in adverse situations and helps them focus on the path forward. Here are some ways to remain positive.

* **Affirmation.** "You have to believe you're good to be good" is a common phrase used in competitive athletics. At the heart of this along with similar statements is the idea of affirmation. An athlete needs to affirm what they are good at and build from that point. For instance, if an athlete has great speed, the affirmation would be "I am fast." It seems rather simple, but student athletes often have difficulty coming up with a simple, accurate, and usable affirmation. "I am the best athlete on my team" is not an affirmation statement. Whether true or not, this type of statement does little to improve performance or team chemistry. Be specific with affirmations ("I am strong," "I am intelligent," "I give great effort," etc.) in order to maintain a positive mindset.

* **Visualization.** You play the game in your mind before you play the game. Athletes should visualize every part of their sport. For instance, for practice, an athlete may visualize getting up early to make their bed, eat breakfast, and arrive early at the practice facility and then visualize themselves giving great effort and attitude during practice. Game day is of particular importance; every aspect of the day should be visualized. The

morning routine, the travel to the venue, the warm-up, the game performance (the positive and possible negative moments) . . . visualize it all. Playing the game in their mind before the game is played helps an athlete keep a positive mindset during the competition.

* **Response.** Athletes should choose how they will respond *before* an event (hard coaching, failure, success, etc.) takes place. Letting your response be decided by your emotions in the moment is not good for anyone and almost guarantees a negative reaction. For instance, when a player makes a mistake, they are coached, sometimes hard. High-level players decide before a mistake how they will handle such correction and remain calm.

* **Words.** Yes, I am using a string of negative words to make my point. Don't use *don't* and other such vocabulary during practice or competition. For instance, saying "Don't let up!" during a break sounds positive but the possibility of "letting up" has just been introduced into the athlete's or team's mindset. It is better to say phrases like, "Keep your foot on the gas!" or "Keep playing your game!" Similarly, yelling at a player "Catch the ball!" after they do just that creates a level of anxiety and fear that is unhelpful to a player's mindset. It is better to say, "Look it in!" with the phrase "Next play!" to offer an actual coaching point and reminder to keep a positive mindset.

* **Compete.** Just play the game, compete. Again, it seems like an easy positive-mindset move, but it can be rather difficult to execute. Why? We compete to win, so we care about the score. If an athlete can focus on each match, at bat, play, or drive, they will perform at

a higher level, and yes, the score will reflect that reality. I have seen many an athlete and team shut down in the first moments of a competition because the score was against them early. The key is to decide to *compete* to the best of your ability each play.

* **Next play.** This is one of the most powerful and simple tools for maintaining a positive mindset. No athlete or team is perfect. Baseball and softball even depend on failure (strikeouts) to proceed to the next inning. Mistakes happen, and yes, some mistakes are bigger than others. Regardless, simply saying to yourself or your team, "Next play!" is a move that reminds the athlete to flush the failed moment and commit to learning, doing better, and moving on to the next competitive moment. It works.

* **Breathe and tap.** Remember, the mind and body are connected. This tool helps the athlete (and parent) remain positive in the most negative of situations. Competition brings out emotion. Emotion that is harnessed and controlled is used for competitive advantage. If emotional control is lost, athletes (and parents) react out of uncontrolled passion, leading to penalties, expulsion, and other censures that hurt both the athlete and team. I use the words *breathe and tap*, others have used the words "Clear the mechanism," to speak of this method for resetting your mind and body for better focus and positive mindset. When you perceive the situation you are in escalating to a negative outcome, take a deep, controlled breath in through the nose and slowly out through the mouth, and then have a physical touch (tap) that serves as a sort of "reset button" for your emotions—breathe and tap.

* **Celebrate and lock (CLK—"Click").** This is my own way of communicating to players and teams to remain up, but not too up, emotionally during competition. When you have the advantage, make the point, score, make a huge defensive play, or capture the momentum, celebrate the moment, but quickly return to an emotionally neutral, focused mindset and, you guessed it, *compete*.

* **One percent better every day.** Typically attributed to the Japanese *Kaizen* method of industry growth, this tool is flooding the athletic psychology literature and helps keep an athlete's mindset positive and growing. The power is in the simplicity. The pathway of long-term, sustained, deliverable improvement begins with a commitment to get 1 percent better at what you are doing each day. Here is how it works. You will not be able to improve your physical assets to the point of first-string status in a week, but you can make progress toward your goal by getting 1 percent better today and tomorrow. Before long, you will increase your chances of becoming a starter. This growth mindset tool is both positive and gives an athlete a trajectory for improvement.

* **Gratitude.** This is perhaps the greatest enemy of negativity. No matter the situation, even if the outcome of their effort is unseen or unrewarded, your student athlete is getting to play a game they love. That gratitude will change a negative mindset into a positive one quickly.

A word to parents. The way you handle your own mindset has a great impact on that of your student athlete.

> If you tend to emotionally lose it at games, so will your kid, or they will shut down emotion altogether.

> If you tend to make excuses or blame others for your failure or lack of opportunity, so will your kid.

> If you tend to complain about everything, so will your kid.

> If you tend to hold on to failure and loss, so will your kid.

> If you tend to think yelling at the coach is your right and winning is all that matters, so will your kid (good luck with the results of that).

I could go on, but the point has been made. Negativity and learning to deal with it is part of life. It is something our student athletes learn from us, the adults. Parents, model a life in which a growing, positive mindset is used to face all challenges, athletic and otherwise. Not one of us is perfect, but the effort will speak volumes to the development of your student athlete in their sport and, more importantly, their human development. Heed this because your student athletes are taking notes.

 **NOW?**

The great thing about mindset is that it can be changed and refined for growth. Practice makes perfect. Here are three practices you can do *now* to help your own and your student athlete's mindset.

## Inventory

Be honest with the type of mindset you have. Considering the definition given at the beginning of this chapter, do you feel you have a *growth mindset*? Why or why not? Are you generally a positive or negative person? How would others who know you answer these two questions?

## Confess

If your inventory brought about areas that need improvement, you may need to make things right with self, parents, students, your coach, or your team. Confession is not a bad thing and is typically defined in terms of forgiveness for sin (rightly so), but it also serves as a way in which you demonstrate your humble desire to get better. Parents, it is all right to confess a bad mindset to your kid and their coach. Student athlete, it is all right to do the same thing and confess to your teammates. Players who confess bad mindset behavior to their coach are not only making a personal statement of growth but demonstrating their ability and willingness to be coached.

## Commit

Whether or not the inventory revealed areas of improvement, commit to protecting and developing a positive growth mindset as a parent or student athlete.

"I am just hurting coach," came the response from this young athlete. Understanding he was playing in the biggest game of his young life and being careful with my words, I spoke with a volume only he could hear, "Then stand tall and go finish the game!"

And he did.

By providing needed pressure and pursuit against the opposing team's high-octane offense, he helped bring about one of the greatest victories in recent school history. One that solidified a share of the district title.

**Mindset matters.**

# PARENTING MATTERS

"It is easier to build strong children than to repair broken men."

—Frederick Douglass

## The "ride home."

A friend shared a story about an exchange between him and his son on the ride home after a game. His son had a rough game and had not played well. My friend started running through the game discussing plays, areas for improvement, and so on. He noticed that his son did not say anything. He asked his son if he was listening, to which his son replied, "I just don't want to talk about the game."

My friend admitted he was irritated by his son's comment and was about to have a firmer conversation when God prompted him, "Shut your mouth!" My friend said at that moment he was reminded of how he felt after a bad game. He obeyed, let silence fill the space, and felt the tension ease instead of pursuing his desire to rehash the game.

The ride home for many athletes looks different based on their performance. It is especially challenging when the parents are the coaches, played the same sport, or played the same position. Parenting matters in sport and helps shape athletes' identities and behaviors. Parents are responsible for *training* their children in all areas, including sport.

**Parenting matters.**

 **WHY?**

I read two articles about parenting, titled "The Ride Home" and "The Car Ride Home."[1] The part that stood out to me was the young athletes' responses to their coach's question about their least favorite part of sport. The athletes answered, "The ride home after the game." Parents' postgame conversations with their children are often well intended, though mistimed.

It is alarming how the ride home after a game profoundly affects athletes, not just youth athletes.[2] The ride home immediately follows the end of the game: win or loss. At this time after a game, emotions remain high, processing is incomplete, frustrations are present, and fatigue is evident.[3]

Despite this reality, parents decide to rehash the game and often compel their child to talk about the game, relive moments of play, and criticize their coaches and teammates. In some cases, parents even force their child to take responsibility for the outcome ("Your team won or lost because of you.") The child's recourse is to embrace that the ride home comes with the territory if they play a sport. Children who decide to persist in sport do so with the understanding that competitive play requires mistimed conversations on their performance as an athlete.

Children who participate in competitive sport are already pushed in a certain direction via the use of long-term athlete development plans. By the time the children hit middle and high school, the system is in full effect and reinforces sport norms and attitudes that uphold athletic values. These do not necessarily mirror parents' values. Think about seventh grade; parents typically no longer coach their children. This is not a bad thing. But the reality is that the "system" has taken the lead in their athletes' development.

Children take cues on what matters to their parents and so, by default, on what should matter to them. The issue is, young athletes do not always have the emotional maturity to bear the weight that comes with parent expectations and sport demands. This can quickly lead a student athlete into burnout.

Organized youth sports should center on *positive, enriching experiences for the children and their parents*.[4] For many children, youth sport often results in a lot of bad experiences that cause young athletes to shut sports out of their lives. The push to develop elite athletes cannibalizes the positives of the sport. Rather than persist in the sport that should have been an enjoyable experience, the athletes leave the sport and everything connected to it. Sadly, this is on the *positive side*.

The worst thing is when youth athletes persist in seeking validation from parents and others through sport. This creates a great tragedy in youth sports. Youth sport burnout and sport abandonment can be avoided in most cases when sport is kept in its proper context: athlete centered and honoring the intent of fun and play. The keys to achieving athlete-centric sport play come down to balance and the right level of parental involvement.

 **HOW?**

Parents are trainers. If you recall, the "Identity Matters" chapter mentioned that the scope of identity investment is equal to the amount of psychological, physical, and emotional energy committed to an athlete's development in their sport. The degree to which the athlete's participation in sport is affirmed by parents, coaches, and teammates reinforces investment in the sport identity role. Sometimes parents intentionally or unintentionally introduce confusion between identities in their young athletes by nurturing and giving priority to sport and giving less attention to other identities and interests such as art and academics.

Parents do not get to outsource training for their children. Parents play visible, vocal, and fixed roles in their children's lives to advocate and promote the *whole* child's interests, including those that do not pertain to sport talent development. The role of parents in the lives of youth involved in sport is twofold: to create an environment where the freedom to explore an interest is nurtured and to promote process-based learning and activity-over-outcome attitudes. Let's look at a couple of examples of how these two roles play out in a real-life scenario.

Joshua Waitzkin,[5] the person behind the 1993 Paramount Pictures film *Searching for Bobby Fischer*, seems to suggest in his book, *The Art of Learning*, that coaches and parents should leverage failure to foster the ability to cope. In David's and my experience in working with athletes, those who were allowed to fail learned to establish healthy relationships with their sport.

When both parent and coach embrace their roles in creating an environment where youth are free to develop their relationship to sport and the promotion of process is elevated above winning, the experience can naturally lead to successful outcomes. Of more importance, a young person need not foreclose on other aspects of their identity by assigning an unhealthy value and relationship to sport that is based on an outcome—"I win; I am a winner," and when "I lose; I must be a loser."[6] Coaches can partner with parents but cannot assume full responsibility for the character development of the athlete.

Again, parents, *training up* your children in all areas, including sport, cannot be outsourced.

## NOW?

Considering the incredible responsibility and impact a parent has on their student athlete, how do we proceed? Here are a few starting places we practice with our young athletes.

### Learn to Be a Fan

A fan is another layer of support. My children participate in competitive sport. Soraya and Asher each started running as part of the Lubbock Olympians Summer Track Club when they were four. Soraya is now ten and Asher eight, and they continue to run for the Olympians, but now as part of USA Track and Field (USATF) and Texas Amateur Athletic Federation (TAAF). Asher also plays basketball. Their athletic abilities and interests in sport are high, but so are their interests in science, art, music, and math. They still fill their idle time with made-up games, which are adorable and a great use of their free time. In short, we have learned and committed to being our kid's biggest fans, on and off the competitive track and court. The key is that their dad and I give equal attention and investment to all their interests and activities. The goal is to let them choose what their relationship with competitive sport looks like and not choose it for them. Learn to be a fan first.

### Encourage Excellence

Soraya and Asher's dad, Marcus, played basketball at a very high level, and I ran track and played basketball in college. The temptation is to steer them in a particular direction. Without focusing on being a fan first, our default steering would be to lead Soraya's and Asher's identities toward that of an athlete.

However, we believe the potential cost is too high to manipulate their identities. Especially since they are so young and puberty has not come, we know their bodies will change, and with those changes come mobility changes and other factors that potentially affect skills. Instead, it is safer to encourage excellence in all they do. Regardless of whether the activity is connected to sport or other non-sport interests, we encourage excellence.

This can be difficult when your kids show signs of being gifted athletically and the gifts beckon to be developed. Parents, we must guard against adult peer pressure early on and remind ourselves to keep what our kids are good at in proper perspective.

## Ask the Right Questions

As mentioned above, the ride home (and other conversations revolving around sport) can be difficult. Asking the right questions leads to better conversation. Here are some suggestions for good *pre*game or *pre*practice questions:

1. Are you ready for your practice/game?
2. How do you feel about the practice/game today?
3. You know this is what you do and not who you are, right?
4. Where do you want to eat afterward?

Here are some suggestions for good *post*game or *post*practice questions:

1. Did you have fun?
2. What did you do well?
3. What do you think you need to work on?
4. What do you want to eat or do you still want to eat?

Any elaboration on any of the questions is determined by them. The goal is to facilitate a safe space for them to walk out of their relationship with sport. My job as a parent is to train them to keep the sport in its proper context and guide them when I sense things getting out of order.

Marcus and I have committed to giving Soraya and Asher a shot at something many elite athletes do not experience: our kids get to choose what their relationship with sport looks like within the context of who God has created them to be. The goal is to teach the kids to hold sport loosely so when it is time to walk away, Soraya and Asher can do so with gratitude, free and clear, knowing that sport is something they did well but was never who they were. Our kids can only hope to achieve this level of freedom in competition if we keep sport in its proper context: it is what you do, not who you are. The context for us is Christ and using sport as a platform to glorify God. We focus on being fans, encouraging excellence, and asking good questions.

I wonder if my friend's son would have gone on to play football in college had my friend made it about the sport over his son in that pivotal moment. I wonder if my friend's desire to love his son more than his son's involvement in sport helped his son develop a healthy relationship with sport. My friend passed the test with his son, which paved the way to get it right with his daughters who are also collegiate athletes.

All three have been able to temper the hold of athlete identity because they were able to form their relationship with sport. This relationship was not determined by their parents but supported by their parents as part of their training process. For my friend, it came down to this important question: "Do I want an athlete, or do I want a relationship with my son that honors God and whom he wants him to be?"

**Parenting matters.**

# REALITY
## MATTERS

"Humankind cannot bear very much reality."

—T. S. Eliot

**"You need to go to the field and see the kid that showed up!"**
These were the excitedly spoken words shared with me as I walked in the field house one summer day. We had been looking for a quarterback to replace the gunslinger we lost to college, and the answer seemed to have dropped on the doorstep of our school. Awesome! Almost.

The eye test of physical appearance. Check.

The athletic ability of speed and strength. Check.

The mental understanding of the game. Check

The emotional ability to control and lead a team. Fail.

All the parts seemed to be in place, but the ability to deal with stressful environments and lead his peers in difficult situations, what coaches refer to as an "x factor," was not present. When placed at the QB position, things could quickly unravel and even turn toxic.

This young man was not the answer to our quarter-back vacancy.

**Reality matters.**

## WHY?

One of the hard truths in competitive athletics, and life in general, is that you can do all the right things in training, commitment, effort, and attitude and *still* not get the prize for which you are striving. One of the greats in Texas high school football coaching, head coach Jay Northcutt of Frenship High School, frequently communicates this truth to his athletes. Follow that up with this grounding statement from Northcutt: "Hard work produces great qualities in life but does not always guarantee a successful outcome. However, what is guaranteed is failure if you do not work hard to achieve your goals." Why are such statements of reality important to a student athlete? The answer is seen in a number of our favorite biblical characters and the moments that defined their *reality*. These three are given as examples.

### Joshua

The leader of Israel who took over after Moses (a tough job with lots of stress) was in the middle of settling the land of promise and was uncertain as to the overall outcome of the campaign. However, he was certain and knew the reality of his decision: "But if serving the LORD seems undesirable to you, then choose for yourselves this day whom you will serve . . . . But as for me and my household, *we will serve the LORD*" (Josh. 24:15—emphasis mine). Joshua had a firm grasp on and commitment to his own reality and the things he truly controlled. Regardless of how his people proceeded, Joshua knew his reality.

## Shadrach, Meshach, and Abednego

The notable companions of Daniel (the lion's den seems to getter better teaching time) faced an incredible moment of reality—certain death—and answered the challenge with their own incredible statement of the reality of their confidence in God. Unwilling to bow their knee and offer godlike praise and allegiance to the ruler they served, the three of them were sentenced to death in a fiery furnace.

The outcome was pretty awesome; but for our purpose, check out their response to the king, "If we are thrown into the blazing furnace, the God we serve is able to deliver us from it . . . . But *even if he does not*, we want you to know, Your Majesty, that we will not serve your gods or worship the image of gold you have set up" (Dan. 3:17–18—emphasis mine). I love this! "Even if he does not," they say to the king, Shadrach, Meshach, and Abednego will not bow their knees. Wow! These three had no idea whether God would rescue them or not. Regardless, reality mattered to these three and would eventually matter to the king they were standing up against.

## Paul

There are many moments worth mentioning in Paul's life, but the one that demonstrates the reality of his mindset is found in the context of recalling his own successes, failures, and obstacles in attaining his life and ministry goals: "*Not that I have already obtained all this*, or have already arrived at my goal, but I press on to take hold of that for which Christ Jesus took hold of me. . . . *I press on* toward the goal to win the prize for which God has called me heavenward in Christ Jesus" (Phil. 3:12, 14—emphasis mine). Paul knew and had confidence in his goal achievement. However, he knew the importance of his own effort and attitude in accomplishing his desired outcome.[1]

What can we learn about reality that translates to student athletes?

**Joshua.** You cannot control how others will respond to your effort and attitude. You can only control you.

**Shadrach, Meshach, and Abednego.** Even when the outcome to your effort and attitude is uncertain, you can remain true to your convictions.

**Paul.** Even when the goal is certain, your thankful response should be seen in your ever-increasing commitment to giving the very best of your attitude and effort.

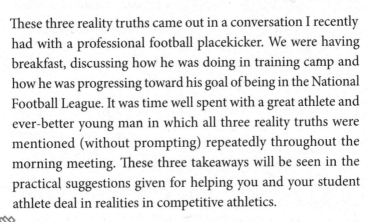

These three reality truths came out in a conversation I recently had with a professional football placekicker. We were having breakfast, discussing how he was doing in training camp and how he was progressing toward his goal of being in the National Football League. It was time well spent with a great athlete and ever-better young man in which all three reality truths were mentioned (without prompting) repeatedly throughout the morning meeting. These three takeaways will be seen in the practical suggestions given for helping you and your student athlete deal in realities in competitive athletics.

## HOW?

It is often difficult to speak in realities with today's competitive athletic families. As mentioned in other places throughout this book, if a student athlete is not given the position, playing time, or "looks" parents believe their kid deserves, conflict can quickly develop.[2] Because it is crucial for acknowledging reality, we are going to go ahead and say the following. Understanding that many of these are helpful, elite team athletic organizations, specialty strength and conditioning coaches and programs, and scouting organizations can create a false reality of success for your student athlete in order to make money and grow their business.[3] In other words, some organizations will say they can help your student athlete get to the next level of play and guarantee looks from scouts if you pay for their program.

To be fair, some of these programs can do just that. But it is possible your student is not getting the help they need. How do you know? Ask great questions! (See "Strength and Conditioning Matters" and ask the same type of questions found in that chapter.) Be sure to have your student talk with their school coach about the organizations. With that said, be willing to hear and consider what the coach may tell you about your student's ability to play at the next level. Here is an example.

I worked as character coach for a competitive high school baseball team in the Dallas–Fort Worth area. A student was cut during tryouts and an angry parent critically called the head coach into account, saying their kid's select team coach said their son could play at the next level and should be on the team. The reality was that the kid did not possess the skills to play at the next level or the high school varsity level. The parent had been sold a reality that was not accurate. No one likes hearing such news, but it helped adjust expectations and set a more realistic outlook for their son's playing future.

Before offering a few how-tos for working realistically with your student athlete's ability to compete, look at the numbers of those athletes who transition from each level of play by going to the referenced websites.[4] The reality is that there is opportunity, but it's limited. Parents, just because your student has success at one level does not assure their success at the next.

**Reality matters.**

## Keeping Your Expectations Realistic

Taken from the truths discovered in the section above, here are some practical ways to help your student athlete, and yourself, navigate competitive athletics with realistic expectations.

***You cannot control how others will respond to your effort and attitude.*** You can only control you. As a student athlete, you are responsible for your own attitude and effort. Your parents cannot manipulate nor control the outcome of that for which you are responsible. If they can, you will eventually be found out, and any success you wish to achieve as an athlete will be destroyed. You control you! Truly, we (Monica and David), wish you the greatest of success in your athletic journey. However, remember, the attitude and effort you give will be that which transforms your trajectory in life. Parents, you can assist your student athlete by getting them into places and positions to be seen and evaluated, but you cannot (nor should you) control their success. As you have seen, very few make it through all levels of competitive athletics.

***Even when the outcome of your effort and attitude is uncertain, you can remain true to your convictions.*** When you buy into the idea that you alone control your own attitude and effort, you are establishing and building a conviction that, no matter the circumstances, you will always give your best. This type of conviction in a competitive athlete guarantees you will get the most out of your physical and emotional assets. It does not guarantee a starting position or success at the next level of play. Regardless, a student athlete can have the satisfaction and fulfillment that they gave their best in pursuit of a goal. This is a commitment that will remain a part of an athlete's lifestyle long after their athletic competition days have ended. That is a gift.

*Even when the goal is certain, your thankful response should be seen in your ever-increasing commitment to giving the very best of your attitude and effort.* If you are an athlete who has gifts to play at the next level and that is what you desire to do, push yourself and continue your growth as an athlete and person. Be the ultimate team player, coachable athlete, and kind of person people want to be around. This will not only increase your "draft" status but "human" status. Remember, our days as athletes will end, so develop the part of you that will last when your competition days are done. Parents, please remind your student athlete that they are seen, loved, and appreciated more for what they do off the field of play.

 **NOW?**

This could be one of the simplest "Now" sections in the book, though it may be one of the most difficult to implement.

### Adjust Expectations

Both parent and athlete can gain a lot by reflecting on these, and similar, questions.

* Do I possess the physical attributes to succeed at this sport?
* Do I possess the mental toughness to succeed at the sport?
* Is my roll on the team as a starter, backup, or practice player?
* Is my lack of success because of my physical and mental ability?
* Is my lack of success because of my attitude and effort?
* What does my coach say about the reality of my place and play on the team?

We want to make it clear that facing *reality* does not mean giving up on competitive athletics. An increase in attitude and effort may indeed increase an athlete's opportunity. Regardless, as mentioned above, an increase in attitude and effort may do nothing more than help an athlete mature in their sport and life. That is a gift. One of the difficulties we see in today's athletic environment is when kids quit athletics after facing the reality that they will never be starters in their sport. Even if you are cut from your team, find ways to compete (recreation leagues, college intramurals, etc.), enjoy the experience, and learn the lessons that come from participating in competitive athletics.

## Make the Most of Reality-Producing Conversations

"You will not play much or any this season, but we want you on the team" is an honest, painful statement spoken to seniors every year by coaches. By their senior season, most student athletes know the reality of the words before they are ever spoken by their coach. *Young athletes who accept these words* push themselves even harder in practice. This helps starters increase their practice level, increases team success, and, at times, results in more, though still limited, playing time. In short, these athletes are a true gift to successful team outcomes and are recognized as such. *Young athletes who do not accept these words* can destroy team dynamics and cause trouble in the locker room. Nothing good comes from such responses. In short, such athletes make excuses and blame others for what could simply be that they have reached the end of their physical abilities.

We may sound like a broken record at this point, but we want competitive athletes to give their greatest effort and attitude toward developing all their athletic gifts. But in the end, your student athlete may have reached or will soon reach their competitive threshold, and that is all right.

☆

We found a quarterback to lead our explosive offense, and it wasn't the physically impressive new arrival. Difficult conversations followed, and we found a position where this student athlete contributed to the team in huge, even clutch, ways; but it wasn't at QB1.

One of the greatest obstacles to finding the right place for this athlete on the team was his parents, who believed his future as a student athlete rested in the quarterback position. Reality was hard to accept and created a bit of tension early in the season. However, once navigated, we had one of the most productive, historic seasons in school history.

And, after accepting the reality of his place on the team. The young man grew and did find a way to play ball at the next level.

**Reality matters.**

# RESPONSIBILITY
## MATTERS

"I am not a product of my circumstances.
I am a product of my decisions."

—Stephen R. Covey

### "You've got to earn it!"

Off-season is a time for athletes to regroup, refocus, and recommit. It is a time to revisit core values, goals, and tasks that, if adhered to, will pay dividends during the season and hopefully result in postseason play. Coaches and athletes alike are aware that the off-season is "seed time" if they want to reap a harvest during the season. Coaches can fashion a plan; but ultimately, the athletes must buy in and take personal and social responsibility to execute tasks that influence outcomes. While visiting a prominent West Texas athletic program, I witnessed my friend Aaron Uzzell, the strength and conditioning coach at Frenship High School and former strength and conditioning coach at Texas Tech, reinforce core values and beliefs that required athletes to bear the consequences of their failure. He expects his players to take personal and social responsibility for the actions that shortchange the efforts needed to make gains.

As Aaron and I talked, a few of the off-season athletes came by the weight room to grab a protein shake but were met with him telling them, "You are out until you guys decide to work. . . . You've got to earn it!" To whom much is given, much is required. This group had a subpar training session and none of them took personal or social responsibility to do their "job." Those jobs are reflected in mantras such as "win the day" or words like *discipline*, *family*, *competition*, and *toughness* that anchor all the tasks implemented in the program. I recognized something much more valuable at play. Aaron, the warden, was teaching these athletes a valuable life principle.

**Responsibility matters.**

 ## WHY?

Responsibility in life is unavoidable and cannot be outsourced. Adults may attempt, intentionally or unintentionally, to mute their student athlete's responsibility in sport, but they do so to the determinant of their student athlete's development of work ethic, ability to fail well, and mental toughness. Lack of responsibility produces a cascade effect that results in a host of problems. Responsibility is inherent in sport participation and supports an athlete's learning.

"How you do sport is how you do life." The first time I heard this phrase, it seemed reductionist at best, because life is much broader in scope and depth than sport. Now I get it. It is not the sport that shapes an athlete's life but the lessons learned through sport participation, like an increased sense of responsibility and ability to cope with life's demands.

One particular life demand is *ownership* of actions and processes that lead to desired outcomes. There is no something for nothing in sports or, more importantly, in life. Sport is a lower-stakes environment for learning and practicing responsibility before the stakes get higher as life progresses.

Aaron demands a sense of responsibility from the athletes in his charge. In a manner of speaking, my friend is teaching his players to "Take up your cross and bear it." There is no proxy or farming out responsibility here in this passage; Christ gives a command. "You pick it up!" Christ is saying to own it, carry it, and be responsible for whatever it is. That is stewardship, a core principle of responsibility.

## HOW?

If responsibility is a necessary ingredient in life to bolster confidence through mental toughness, grit in struggle and challenge, persistence and perseverance, and enthusiasm as a byproduct of achievement, why not reinforce tasks that lend themselves to teaching responsibility? In the opening story, the phrase "personal and social responsibility" was used repeatedly. These two types of responsibility play critical roles in completing the tasks that yield achievement.

### Personal Responsibility

Personal responsibility is demonstrated in the hard work, intrinsic motivation, commitment, time management, and mental toughness associated with sports play. Taking personal responsibility promotes confidence when athletes fully embrace and are held accountable to the standard of excellence needed to excel in their sport. Failure plays an essential role in the development of personal responsibility. Failure requires the individual to decide whether to learn and persist or make excuses and remain. The worst response to failure is to quit. We discussed in the "Failure Matters" chapter that failure is not fatal but rather a catalyst for growth. When parents and student athletes decide to embrace failure, both groups will understand the gifts failure brings to athletic and life growth. This is the nature of responsibility—*I own my role to meet the demand.*

## Social Responsibility

Social responsibility is demonstrated in a strong team chemistry. The locker room is a place the student athlete wants to spend time. Words like *family, character,* and *tradition* are used in places where social responsibility is emphasized, such as the hallway in an athletic training facility I walk through on occasion. Social responsibility is also demonstrated through tough coaching. Aaron refused protein shakes to those who did not meet the standard of work. He was reinforcing not only personal but social responsibility.

How are personal and social responsibilities developed? To parents and athletes, it typically looks like hard, demanding, often loud coaching. This is not random "coaching" stuff. It is strategic and part of a process called *time under tension.*

## Time under Tension

Time under tension is a training term used in exercise physiology (strength and conditioning) and refers to the process that leads to muscle hypertrophy (a fancy word for growth). The load placed on the muscle causes the central nervous system to divert resources to adapt to the load. The result of "time under tension" is muscle growth and an increase in strength. It's science and it works. This process is repeated several times, in various ways, to develop an athlete's strength and speed; all of which is translated into a higher level of competition in their given sport. This principle works in life, too. The entire premise behind neuroplasticity, or growth mindset, works the same.

Mental toughness, a familiar term used in athletics, is developed through time under tension. Mental toughness increases when meeting challenges.

 **NOW?**

What can parents do to promote personal and social responsibility using time under tension? Asking parents to encourage their student athletes to take responsibility and own the process (which includes failure) calls for calculated moves that take discernment to achieve a desired outcome. Below are a few practical ways to safely help your student athlete develop personal and social responsibility.

### Listen

When your student athlete tells you, or you find out, about a situation with a tough "responsibility" coaching moment, do not be quick to side with them or provide an out. Listen and ask how they might address the situation. Listening is about gauging and learning how your student athlete is responding to a situation. The goal is to listen and learn to steer the athlete in the right direction. Again, do not provide an easy way out and waste time-under-pressure learning opportunities.

### Learn

We all have a default setting, which according to Marten's 1975 Personality Pyramid is reflected in our typical responses to situations.[1] Learn to recognize your student athlete's typical responses regarding difficult situations. Typical responses can include avoidance, anger, disinterest, obsession, stress, and excuses, all of which are understandable but detrimental should the student athlete remain in that state. Learning helps parents forecast their student athlete's typical response so they can assign the appropriate reaction to teach themselves and their athletes how to lean into the right character-building practice for difficult situations.

## Lean

Lean into long-term character investment using microlessons that deal with responsibility. For example, when an issue arises between your student athlete and a coach, be slow to intervene where there is not an imminent threat. Rather, encourage your student athlete to have a conversation with the coach to gain understanding and own their role in the issue. Tips on how to help your student have a conversation with their coach can be found in "Conflict Matters" and "Coaching Matters."

This L³ Approach (listen, learn, and lean) should enable parents to partner with their athletes to promote self-regulation and self-awareness that lead to greater levels of the responsibility and sense of ownership required to work through issues in athletics and, here it comes, in life.

Teach responsibility—life principles—to athletes.

As I stood in the back of the facility, watching and listening to the head coach address the team on matters of mindset and habits that influence work ethic, one coach explained to me that some athletes come hardwired with commitment and the enthusiasm needed to work hard and own the process. The coach added that for several of the athletes, especially nowadays, such skills and mindsets must be drawn out of athletes through conditioning.

The coach stated that "conditioning includes repeating and defining anchor terms like *discipline*, *family*, and *standard* that are foundational values that shape the program." Coach continued to share how personal and social responsibility is enforced and reinforced with extrinsic rewards for each athlete's commitment and persistence in owning tasks that will lead to success. Interestingly, I saw a few athletes with the protein shakes that were not given to the first group.

The athletes with the protein shakes beamed as they drank them while the head coach talked. Later, I asked about the group with the shakes, and my friend simply stated, "They earned it." What a simple but powerful lesson; personal and social responsibility are an intrinsic choice to commitment. It comes from within. For those athletes, it was not about the shake; it was about the effort, and they had earned it.

**Responsibility matters.**

# STRENGTH AND CONDITIONING MATTERS

"If the decisions you make about where you invest your blood, sweat, and tears are not consistent with the person you aspire to be, you'll never become that person."

—Clayton M. Christensen

I was a two-sport student athlete in track and basketball. I left sport prematurely for reasons I will not get into—though the reasons would make a great book. One summer, I decided to pick a basketball up in the hope of playing competitively. First tournament and second game, I ruptured my patellar tendon—the big one that attaches to the quad and shin and holds the kneecap in place, yeah that one.

I underwent surgery to repair the tendon and had to be in an immobilizer for six weeks at zero flexion (a fancy way of saying don't bend it). Six weeks is a long time to think about how the body you spent so much time developing to meet and exceed the demands of your sport has failed you. Six weeks seems an eternity to sit with the question, "Will I ever be able to return to sport again?"

Ten weeks post-op, I paid my *now* friend Aaron Uzzell, who was then the strength and conditioning (S&C) coach at Texas Tech, a visit. Aaron happened to be in the entrance hallway to the football training facility the moment I walked in on crutches. He yelled, "Leave your crutches at the door!"

My first thought was, "He knows I am just ten weeks post-op, right?" Followed by, "I can't walk without my crutches." For whatever reason, I left my crutches at the door and dragged my injured self and low confidence toward my S&C friend. Physically and emotionally broken, I did what he said.

**Strength and conditioning matters.**

## WHY?

"I pray that you may prosper in all things and be in good health, just as your soul prospers" (3 John 2 NJKV). God deals in the whole and not parts. It makes sense that we see ourselves in the same light—as a whole. For an athlete at any level, the emphasis on physical wholeness for performance's sake is crucial. Proper training is often unattended to until injuries and a performance lapse occur.

Think about the length and rigor of a competitive season. If most athletes start playing competitive sports around six years old, that is a lot of time. Then consider how many competitors play year-round. Do the math. How many games is that in a calendar year? Now think about how much physical load and wear on the body that is in a calendar year. Wow!

Dr. Fraze and I often hear parents say, "Well, they're young and can handle it!" Even, "My kid wants to play year-round; she loves it!" Most of the time when we hear these phrases, it is often an attempt to justify an athlete's year-round play. We concede the fact that each of these statements might be true.

We simply want athletes and parents to ask, "What are the possible short- and long-term costs of such stress?"

I want you to consider two verses. "'I have the right to do anything,' you say—but not everything is beneficial" (1 Cor. 6:12), and, "Suppose one of you wants to build a tower. Won't you first sit down and estimate the cost to see if you have enough money to complete it?" (Luke 14:28). Of course these verses give practical wisdom for spiritual measurement. However, they also provide a way to evaluate the consequences for involvement in year-round sport.

Parents must account for cumulative load and fatigue with that much play. Monitoring, moderating, and training are the only means to combat the cumulative load of year-round intensity in sport participation. Right now, we will just deal with training as a moderator.

 **HOW?**

Year-round play places athletes at the higher end of physiological stress and strain. This is compounded by academic, peer, social, interscholastic, and club/select sport stressors. The body does not compartmentalize stressors. In short, all stress flows into one bucket. Then add that three-quarters of the athletes Dr. Fraze and I are referencing in this book have a training age of zero. *Training age* equals the years an athlete has been trained by a *competent* strength and conditioning coach.

Training is not merely going to practice, learning plays, and so on. Training is about tactically manipulating the central nervous system to increase strength, power, endurance, agility, and durability through strength and conditioning practices. (We are not getting into exercise physiology or science stuff, so do not stop reading!) These practices, if properly incorporated into training methods, should support injury prevention and result in peak performance. However, the key to practice is the S&C coach.

 ## NOW?

Many strength and conditioning professionals claim to be competent. Parents, coaches, and athletes may be at a loss in selecting such a professional. As in any profession, all skills are not equal. But a good S&C coach should be able to demonstrate a track record of high-performing, durable athletes who buy into the process.

In my work with injured athletes, I have been asked by athletes and parents, "Where do we start to get back to playing?" I start with a return to sport (RTS) plan and then share how to find and vet a competent S&C coach. I will flip the order in this chapter and share how to find and vet an S&C coach first. There are a few things to consider when vetting an S&C professional. Interview them and ask the following:

* What is your training or certification?
* What is your experience?
* Whom have you worked with that I might know?
* How many noncontact injuries have happened on your watch?
* May I speak to some of your athletes and parents?
* Aaron's favorite question: Can you [S&C coach] show validity for what you do?
* How do you get to know your athletes?
* Do you have or will you develop a relationship or communicate with their coaches or other professionals the athlete works with?

Another thing to consider in selecting a coach is whether the athletes they work with pass the "eye test." Meaning, do the athletes look and move like "athletes"? Go and watch the training sessions. You can also ask athletes who have worked with the S&C coach similar questions:

* How long have you worked with them?
* How did you get connected with them?
* Why do you like working with this coach?
* How much access do you have to the coach outside of training sessions?
* Did they do your RTS? If so, what was that like?
* What are some of the things they told you during the RTS process? (Listen for confidence-building language/conversations.)

Finally, *do not* take your friends and other athletes' or families' endorsements of the S&C coach without talking to the coach. This may seem like a lot of questions. This is not even an exhaustive list of questions that I would normally recommend athletes and parents ask S&C coaches. Think of it this way: you would not buy a car without taking it for a test drive. Maybe you would, but let's be more critical before we give folks access to our athletes (our children).

## Recommendations for Injured Athletes

Athletic injuries can be devasting. Athletes have reported depression, anxiety, insomnia, hopelessness, identity loss, obsessive tendencies, withdrawal, aggression, and lack of interest in other activities, such as academics, when an athletic injury occurs.[1] Despite the reality of these factors, athletes, parents, and coaches can constructively navigate this challenging time. Here is how.

*Manage perspective.* Everything in life is a matter of perspective: "As he thinks in his heart, so is he" (Prov. 23:7 NKJV). There are four strategies that frame perspective:

* **Goal setting.** Athletes should participate in developing, evaluating, and amending the treatment and return to sport plans. The goal of the plans should anchor the process.

* **Visualization/mental rehearsal/mental imagery (VI/MR/MI).** VI/MR/MI involves focusing on mental images of a task along with other associated senses without physically performing the task. Athletes, performers for that matter, use VI/MR/MI in low-stakes settings, before competition or practice, to prepare for higher-stakes settings. This strategy incorporates motivational aspects in goal orientation and arousal and cognitive factors like skills and strategy.[2]

* **Self-talk (ST).** Self-talk, simply stated, denotes how we communicate with ourselves to sway or shape "thoughts, feelings, and behaviors."[3] Athletes locate their perception of how they are dealing with injury by what they are saying to themselves. Here are a few recommendations for creating and maintain productive self-talk:

  * *Be real.* Accept that you are injured. Stay positive. This is a choice.

  * *Cue.* I have encouraged some of my RTS athletes to write down phrases that "cue" them to deploy positive ST. Some phrases include "Keep working," or "One more set," and even, "Keep it moving."

  * *Trust your team.* Your confidence in the plan, process, and return to playing is increased when

you trust the professionals working with you. Remember, you may have to borrow their confidence until you can reestablish your own.

- ⊚ *Goal setting.* Revisit the first perspective-management strategy. This is not a time to be passive. Be part of *your* recovery and RTS process.
- ⊚ *Ask questions.* Be informed about the injury and rehabilitation process.
- ⊚ *Incorporate visualization/mental rehearsal/mental imagery.* You may want to work with a credible mental performance coach to facilitate this process.
- ⊚ *Increase your IQ.* Make good use of the time. Learn more about your sport, your position, and the other positions while you are off the field.
- ⊚ *Don't forget you are still part of your team.* Be a supportive teammate.
- ⊚ *Focus.* You can control your effort. Give attention to that in training and mental performance sessions.
- ⊚ *Celebrate the smallest wins.* Do not go overboard, but use wins and gains to boost confidence.
- ✳ **Arousal control.** Arousal is a combination of psychological and physiological aspects of the motivation people experience. The key is optimal arousal not only in competition but during rehabilitation and RTS. Stress and anxiety rob focus and energy needed for high-quality training.

These four strategies work together to steer perspective. They work. If they did not, the military would not use these and similar strategies to train special operators. Use them, athletes. I currently use them in my own life, with my kids, and with the athletes and business professionals I work with. Henry Ford

Health also offers helpful tips for injured athletes worth considering.[4] Another often overlooked strategy is to have a return to sport plan.

***Return to Sport.*** I cannot tell you how many athletes returning from an injury express their concern as to whether they are ready and able return to their sport. Most of the uncertainty stems from a breakdown in one of the four strategies listed above and a lack of "testing" the injury through an RTS protocol. I ask these timid athletes, "What was your RTS?" Most of the athletes describe a process that is not even close to a rehabilitation RTS plan:

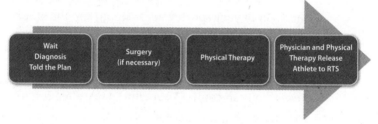

What is missing? The RTS protocol. Aaron Uzzell was responsible for RTS at my alma mater. When athletes were cleared by the physician and physical therapist, they would go to Aaron. Aaron would spend the next two to three weeks reconditioning the athlete for the physical and positional demands of their prospective sport. An indirect benefit of RTS is that the athlete had little or no doubt that they would be ready to compete at a high level. RTS promoted confidence because the athlete was able to "test" the repair and assess how it would hold up under the demand.

I ultimately "left my crutches at the door," and it was confusing because it didn't seem like he understood I was hurt.

I was only able to leave my crutches because I borrowed Aaron's confidence. Why did he demand I leave the crutches? Because he knew I had to psychologically break from seeing myself as injured and all that comes with that fatalistic mindset. Strength and conditioning and return to sport coaching is bigger than just checking the box that an athlete can run and jump again. It enables the athlete to recondition and retrain for the physical demands of their sport and regain the mental confidence needed for reentry into competition.

**Strength and conditioning matters.**

# TRANSITION MATTERS

"I might have had a tough break;
but I have an awful lot to live for."

—Lou Gehrig

I have three stories.

*First story*. I recently heard from a former student athlete asking about how to request official transcripts to send to another university so this individual's remaining eligibility could be vetted. This student had been to four different colleges and universities to play baseball and was still making efforts to play.

Before this student transferred, he shared that he did not know what he would do once he could no longer play. I recall that during a class discussion, this former student athlete had shared that his parents spent "easily one hundred thousand dollars" on baseball-related activities (training, traveling, private lessons, league fees and membership). All investment was focused on his persisting in baseball, not life after baseball.

*Second story.* A few years ago, a student athlete, who was struggling with a chronic medical condition, shared a desire to walk away from competitive sport. Sport had begun to take a toll on this athlete's body and mental health, compounding the chronic condition. The athlete wanted to quit for a while, but one of the athlete's parents did not approve and threatened to have the student cover the cost of school should they quit. In this instance, the student athlete's inability to leave sport was not their own doing but the result of the parent's inability to cut ties with their identity as the "parent of a student athlete."

*Third story.* I know a person who pursued basketball for many years, well into their thirties, to the detriment of developing other identities, interests, and skills. This individual played basketball in Europe, South America, and the Middle East, finishing their professional career in the States. The offers slowed, but their desire did not subside at the same pace. Participation in sports is terminal, and all efforts to resuscitate a failing career impacted this person's ability to transition into a role that would support their long-term needs and responsibilities to family and future.

Each of the stories deals with transition—transition for the student athlete and, in some instances, for the parents. It is hard to move on from something that plays a large role in shaping and reinforcing identity, such as sport.[1] A healthy exit from sport requires a plan.

**Transition matters.**

 **WHY?**

The demands associated with competitive sports support a hyperfocus on skill development and can result in an athlete foreclosing on or delaying the pursuit of interests, hobbies, career exploration, and professional development needed to transition from their sport when the time comes. In the chapter "Identity Matters," the concept of identity foreclosure was introduced as the agent behind athletic identity. Athletic identity means individuals accept and embrace their athlete roles and ignore other aspects of their identity needed to successfully leave the sport and excel in other arenas.

Interestingly, parents, coaches, and athletes mistakenly believe that a singular focus on sports will make the athlete better. In reality, the athlete will perform better when they are encouraged to bring the fullness of who they are to their sport (i.e., they win more competitions). The reason for expanding focus to other interests for the individual is simple: *they are more than just an athlete.* This simple realization enables the athlete to play freely and leave the sport freely, taking all they have learned from sport with them into the next arena. Otherwise, the consequences of an out-of-balance athletic identity mean the athlete's involvement in sport is the respirator and they fail to breathe without it.[2] The Bible would call that *idolatry.*

"Do not worship any other god, for the LORD, whose name is Jealous, is a jealous God" (Exod. 34:14). This commandment is part of the Lord's Top Ten. On its face, some might think God sounds a bit narcissistic, but that is far from the case. God's heart is for us and for us to have a healthy relationship with him. What we "worship" is evidenced in the relationships we have with others and in what we do. He is for his children, just the way they are, and walks with his children into what they were created to be in Christ. Sport, namely competitive sport, has the power to undermine his intent. This happens when athletes, coaches, and parents fail to keep the sport in proper context: *sport is what I do and not who I am.*

Sport can skew a student athlete, especially an elite athlete, toward an identity that can and often does conflict with God's will for us.[3] Sport performance becomes an idol, an idol demanding our first fruits (the Lord is supposed to get those). The skew toward sport becomes a snare. In Proverbs, the word "snare" is used repeatedly, "Fear of man will prove to be a snare, but whoever trusts in the LORD is kept safe" (Prov. 29:25). The intent of a snare is to trap, confine, or restrict. Athletic identity can have the same effect on individuals who hyperembrace their role as an athlete. They become trapped, confined, and restricted from exploring the fullness of who they are apart from sport and, most importantly, who they are created to be in Christ. Both of which support a healthy transition from sport.

In short, any transition out of sport is or will be difficult because of the time and effort placed into sport. When sport becomes an idol, that transition is much more difficult to manage.

 ## HOW?

It would be great if balance in sport was an automatic process, but it is not. If it were, quite frankly, there would be no need for this book. Since there is a need for this book, let's outline how we address imbalances that lead to difficult transitions from sport. Our process centers around developing and supporting a healthy relationship with sport.

### Develop a Healthy Relationship with Sport

In the "Parenting Matters" chapter, I shared our kids' high interests in sports and how Marcus and I create balance through efforts to give equal attention and investment to all their interests and activities. Again, the goal is to let the kids choose what their relationship with competitive sports looks like and not choose it for them. There is always the temptation to guide them in a direction we choose. If not intentional, our default steering would lead Soraya's and Asher's identities toward that of an athlete. So the goal for us as parents is to check ourselves first and see how and where any conversations about sports are oriented.

In our opinion, those orientations must be about leveraging sport to support kingdom lessons and service. Those lessons come with messages like, "Whatever you do, whether in word or deed, do it all in the name of the Lord Jesus, giving thanks to God the Father through him" (Col. 3:17), and other kingdom principles for how to work hard and focus on your goals, such as "run with perseverance the race marked out for [you]" (Heb. 12:1). Both verses direct my heart as a mother toward the Father first so I can help my children do the same. Admittedly, the choice to stay kingdom-focused in competitive sports is not easy and is a day-to-day, practice-to-practice, and game-to-game decision for parents and, candidly, for coaches and athletes as well. This is especially true when the person is gifted athletically. The goal is to keep things in proper perspective.

Transition issues from sport impact individuals at all levels. Have you ever sat with a young athlete who did not make the travel team or was cut from select or club? Their experience has the same weight as a collegiate or professional athlete who is injured, at the end of their eligibility, has lost a scholarship or contract, or any other situation that undermines their ability to do the thing that gives them identity. For this reason, transition conversations are critical at any level of sports competition to get the performer looking forward.

## Develop a Plan for Life after Sport

The hope is to assist your athlete to consider and plan for life beyond sport. This is best done incrementally rather than abruptly, which often creates an anxiety-laden situation in the mindset of an athlete. The goal is to have similar interest conversations that lead to transition plans that support and promote career exploration, professional development, and a healthy departure from competitive play. In short, talk about and help your athlete plan for the future in all areas.

 **NOW?**

Transition planning should run concurrent with participation in sports. It needs to be an "as we go" conversation. Without intentional focus from parents, the lack of transition conversations could lead to identity foreclosure and the rooting of an athletic identity that is unbalanced, unhealthy, and destructive to the athlete. Unbalanced identities show when the individual understands the value of their identity based solely on athletic performance, social cues, and the need to define themselves as an athlete. Commit to reminding your kid they are much more than an athlete.

Support your students' athletic pursuits but balance this with who they want to become apart from sport. Certainly, this involves future vocation choices, but at the core, center all discussions on their identity as a child of God.

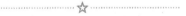

The ESPN 30 for 30 documentary *Broke* chronicles current and former professional athletes who, despite earning millions, have gone broke playing sports. The interview with Jamal Mashburn starkly contrasted the others in the documentary. Mashburn said, "I am more fulfilled and intellectually stimulated now than when I played." Throughout the documentary, Mashburn spoke of plans and ventures that ran concurrently (sound familiar?) with his time as a professional athlete and helped ease his exit from professional sport. He spoke of his time in sports with gratitude and appreciation for what sports taught and afforded him but seemed to know while he was playing that "lacing them up" would end. He seemed to be the only one in the documentary who prepared for and knew this practical truth.

**Transition matters.**

# CHURCH MATTERS

"You are true athletes when you prepare yourselves
not only by training your bodies but also by constantly
engaging the spiritual dimensions of your person for a
harmonious development of all your talents."

—John Paul II

"Your attendance numbers on Wednesday night are going down," my executive minister stated before following up with the sincere and curious question, "What's the problem?"

This type of question is often perceived by youth ministry professionals as a threatening inquiry signaling the end of a ministry. This one was different. The executive had confidence in our ministry. They just had trouble understanding where the students had gone.

This inquiry led to a series of conversations with other churches, youth leaders, and school administrators. What was the overarching conclusion? Every youth ministry's Wednesday

---

This chapter is an extension of Chapter 1, "Balance Matters," and written specifically for those who are wanting to make church activity a priority in their athletic journey.

night church activity was in decline. The culprit seemed to be athletic practice and competition (as well as band, theater, and other competitive extracurriculars). In short, Wednesday nights were no longer protected and sacred. Our athletes were missing. What followed was a reimagining, a creative development in youth ministry programming.

**Church matters.**

## WHY?

"We are going to have to miss _____ (church, retreat, mission trip, camp, Bible study, etc.) because of the game, practice, or tournament . . ." are words all too often spoken by student athletes and parents. It seems like the more competitive the athlete, the more often these words are spoken. Parents want to support every opportunity their student athlete has to improve their game. This is not a bad thing in and of itself. However, without intentional planning on the part of families, missing the occasional church gathering can turn into missing all gatherings. Why is it important for student athletes and families to remain active in church? Here is why.

> Teenagers are part of the church. As such, youth ministry programming should be carried out in the context of the wider church community. Within this community, so much of what a teenager wants and needs is provided.

>> Just as a body, though one, has many parts, but all its many parts form one body, so it is with Christ. For we were all baptized by one Spirit so as to form one body—whether Jews or Gentiles, slave or free—and we were all given the one

Spirit to drink. Even so the body is not made up of one part but of many. . . .

But in fact God has placed the parts in the body, every one of them, just as he wanted them to be. If they were all one part, where would the body be? As it is, there are many parts, but one body.

The eye cannot say to the hand, "I don't need you!" And the head cannot say to the feet, "I don't need you!" On the contrary, those parts of the body that seem to be weaker are indispensable, and the parts that we think are less honorable we treat with special honor. And the parts that are unpresentable are treated with special modesty, while our presentable parts need no special treatment. But God has put the body together, giving greater honor to the parts that lacked it, so that there should be no division in the body, but that its parts should have equal concern for each other. If one part suffers, every part suffers with it; if one part is honored, every part rejoices with it. (1 Cor. 12:12–14, 18–26)

I have included this rather long passage for a reason. Slow down and read this section of Scripture again. Notice that inclusion, purpose, value, and support are themes that run through Paul's discussion on the church. These are all qualities that a teenager wants and needs and that can be found in the community of the church.

> Teach the older men to be temperate, worthy of respect, self-controlled, and sound in faith, in love and in endurance.
>
> Likewise, teach the older women to be reverent in the way they live, not to be slanderers or addicted to much wine, but to teach what is good. Then they can urge the younger women to love their husbands and children, to be self-controlled and pure, to be busy at home, to be kind, and to be subject to their husbands, so that no one will malign the word of God.
>
> Similarly, encourage the young men to be self-controlled. In everything set them an example by doing what is good. In your teaching show integrity, seriousness and soundness of speech that cannot be condemned, so that those who oppose you may be ashamed because they have nothing bad to say about us. (Titus 2:2–8)

When Paul spoke to Titus concerning the teaching of appropriate doctrine, young and old were intentionally mentioned together. He expected the young and old to be in dynamic relationship within the church in order to ensure that a holy lifestyle was maintained. To be clear, I am not advocating we shut down youth ministry programming. On the contrary, there is great benefit found in letting each generation process, challenge, educate, and find support within their own peer groups. However, this should not be done at the exclusion of intergenerational connection.[1]

Because age-specific programming draws a crowd, it is difficult to see why exclusively separating age groups for ministry programming is a bad idea. To be fair, each age group is getting their needs met on their own level. That is good. Right?

Let's take a two-question quiz:

* How many sermons, lessons, and programming moments (camp, retreat, conference, etc.) do you remember that impacted your spiritual life?
* How many adult relationships do you remember that impacted your spiritual life?

I am certain that you can recall more people than programs. It's not that youth ministry programming is inconsequential, but you probably remember adults who made those programs so impactful and memorable.[2]

If the church community has such great importance in the spiritual development of a teenager, it is imperative that church participation and activity remain a priority in the life of competitive athletic families. Without intentional planning, the demands of athletic involvement can overwhelm church participation.[3] No matter what you are told, the church does and should matter in the life of your competitive student athlete and family.

## HOW?

How to handle the demands on time created by both athletic involvement and church involvement is one of the questions most frequently asked by families. It is an appreciated question and demonstrates the athletic family's desire to remain balanced in both worlds.

## Reframing the Debate

Before giving a few practical suggestions, let's refocus this question and give validity to the struggle.

***Missing a church activity may be the most "spiritual" thing you can do as an athlete and family.*** What? You heard me correctly. When you join a team, you are making a commitment to participate and support those you are competing with. This presents a great opportunity to model good sportsmanship and character. It also gives your family an opportunity to share your faith with others (see below).

***Missing a church activity may be a demonstration and development of your student athlete's leadership ability and potential to influence their peers for Christ.*** Remember the "Wednesday night church is no longer sacred" statement? What we, youth ministers, started to understand within this new reality is that our competitive athletic kids, instead of being made to feel guilty for their absence, could be trained and encouraged to use this leadership opportunity to show and reflect Christ in their schools. In other words, if these students are being looked to for leadership in church, why would they not be that in their mission field of competitive athletics?

## Managing the Tension

These two realities help reshape the question of time demands created by church and competitive athletic involvement. With that said, considering the need (perceived or not) we have for church involvement, the reframing is not an excuse to simply not participate. The opposite is true; the more you serve as a "missionary" athlete and family in competitive athletics, the more you need church. Here are some suggestions for remaining intentional with church activity.

***Know the expectations before committing.*** Do not be enamored by the winning program or coach. Know at the beginning what is expected. Most, if not all, athletic programs give a calendar and list of expectations for athletes and families. Read the fine print, talk to others about the "unspoken/unwritten" expectations, ask questions at information meetings, and make sure you feel comfortable with the demands placed on your time and commitment to that time. Some good questions:

* How many absences can my athlete have before their playing time is impacted?
* If my athlete goes to their church's summer camp or mission, will they be treated differently?
* How many weekends are going to be impacted by my athlete's participation?

While each program's and state's rules for competition can be different, it has been our experience that most high-level programs understand the time taken by mission trips or camp experiences. Yes, there may be "make up" work expected to compensate for the week(s) of work lost, but that opportunity is given out of respect for their religious convictions. Pro tip: If your student athlete demonstrates a consistent, above-reproach work ethic in practice and play, absence for church activity is easier to work with and around.

***Be creative and sacrificial with your calendar.*** Sacrifice is a word used in sport across the world. As illustrated in the opening story of "Balance Matters," a sacrifice of your time and "driving time" could eliminate many of the obstacles faced by athletic families regarding their calendars. Let's be clear. It is a sacrifice. It is one worth making so your athlete remains connected to church activity. Creativity is also a skill that was illustrated in that opening story. Of course, it depends on your student athlete's sport, position, and responsibilities, and knowing when your student is actually needed for play is helpful in adjusting your busy calendar. Creativity will demand having respectful conversation(s) with your coach.

***Offer worship gatherings.*** If you are missing your church worship gatherings because of a sport weekend, offer a gathering for families who want to make church activity a priority. If you need assistance in doing this type of inviting or resources for planning a gathering, reach out to your church pastor or Fellowship of Christian Athletes representative.[4]

***Don't forsake the assembly.*** In the end, commit to church activity! There are times when athletic families have no team, training, or game play commitments on Sundays or other church activity times. They simply choose not to participate, taking time to rest. I get it. I really do. Life, whether you are involved in competitive athletics or not, is busy, and Sunday can be seen as an optional activity. Fight this temptation.

> And let us consider how we may *spur one another on* toward love and good deeds, not giving up meeting together, as some are in the habit of doing, but *encouraging one another*—and all the more as you see the Day approaching. (Heb. 10:24–25— emphasis mine)

Did you notice my italicized phrases? We need *one another*! Church matters to your athlete and family.

## NOW?

By this point in the chapter, you can see our passion and belief that church matters in the life of a competitive athlete and their family. It takes intentionality to recast the relationship of church and athletic activity. It takes intentionality to keep church activity a priority. Both begin with a simple and significant decision; *commit* to making church a priority! The execution of this commitment may take some undoing and hard conversations with your student athlete and coach or organization. But it is crucial. Crucial!

"Can I bring a bunch of students to Wednesday night church after practice?"

"Of course," was my response! Of course! These students came from a local high school, and the question was from a dedicated community mom who wanted these kids involved with church activity. "Can we keep a few pizzas for those who arrive late?"

"Of course!" came the response.

They came. A lot of students came because church activity was reimagined. "We are going to hang around a little longer before and after youth group, if any of you can join us," was the request I made to our youth staff and Wednesday night volunteers. Sometimes students who were unable to make the Wednesday night worship activity could make it before or after for hang out time. We wanted to provide motivated adults to connect with them and let them experience "church" before or after their practice or game.

Get this, at times adult volunteers would miss Wednesday night programming to attend and support one of our students as they competed.

Why go to all the trouble?

Why not serve those who come and make them adapt to your schedule?

Simple.

**Church matters.**

# CONCLUSION

I still remember my *last play*.

Home game, full stands, bright lights, band playing, and the sound of that final whistle. I turned toward the crowd and took a mental picture. A picture I can recall clearly and remains with me to this day.

Our (Monica's and David's) "playing days" are over, but we are unable to forget the lessons, good and bad, that came from being involved in competitive athletics. As we tell current athletes, the words and events from those playing days continue to encourage, direct, and challenge us. The words of coaches rattle in our heads. The lessons learned from moments of success and failure continue to teach. It is a gift. A precious gift.

A lot of life has happened since that *last play*. A *lot* of life. Through all the ups and downs, while our foundation and identity are set on who we are in Christ Jesus, much of the grit and determination to *survive* and *thrive* in life came from our playing days.

We pray this book has provided helpful and practical advice as you navigate today's often complicated and confusing world of competitive athletics.

How do you know if your journey was successful?

Whatever level of play you achieve, when your *last play* comes, if you can look back with gratitude, with your identity set on who you are apart from your sport, and with lessons learned rattling around in your head, you have been successful.

# In Their Own Words

The following are responses to the question, "What is the most important thing you would like to share with young athletes and parents of athletes?" The responses validate the need for the information found in each chapter. We list them with no content changes or context to highlight the passion and point each contributor is making. Countless years of experience and involvement as and with athletes, families of athletes, and sport are represented in the next few pages. There is a lot of practical wisdom given by individuals. Read, reflect, and be challenged.

"Playing sports is fun! I believe that as a young athlete, you should play as many as you can. Each sport will develop skills to help you in everything you do. As a parent, you should always remember your child is watching you! Sports are fun and build friendships that will last a lifetime."

—**Kirby Hocutt** (Director of Athletics, Texas Tech University)

"There are so many things young athletes and their parents need to know that it would take years to list them all. This book is the first step to a winning formula for this process. The first word that came to mind after reading the question was 'faith.' A family that has a solid foundation in their respective faith will always be there for each other. Parents are the first and last influencers to see their children. Not a coach, not their teammates. Parents need to motivate, discipline, and support their children. It's like making pizza. The family and its faith are the crust that holds it together. The coaches add the toppings. But without the crust, it falls apart. I believe in FAD: faith, accountability, and discipline. This is a great formula for pizza."

—**Brian Couso** (Former NBA Scout for the Los Angeles Clippers, Part Owner of The Map Sports Facility, Head Coach Nike/NBA Summer Pro League Coach, Servite HS Varsity Coach)

"Athlete . . . find your passion and go with it as far as you can. You will have coaches who are great and some not so great. Learn from both.

"Parents . . . let your athlete find their passion, then feed it! Cheer for *all* the kids, not just your own, and refrain from talking negatively about coaches or officials in front of your athlete."

—**Brad Fichtel** (NFL Alumni, Texas High School Coach)

"The most important thing that I would tell young athletes and parents is to remember what athletics and the University Interscholastic League are designed to do. The purpose of athletics is to help the education process of molding young students by teaching them hard work, trust, competitiveness, dedication, being a valuable part of a team, and the processes of building a team. Too many times, the goal of being in extracurricular athletics is to earn a scholarship, which for a vast majority of athletes will not happen."

—**Del Van Cox** (Assistant Athletic Director, Abilene ISD)

"Support your athlete in *their* dream. Set boundaries with your athlete on topics of discussion (coaching tips, strategy, account-ability, etc.) and time of discussions (right after competition, twenty-four hour rule, no discussions during the car ride home, etc.). Do not question or criticize their coach (the coach will never have their respect or buy-in if the parent criticizes them to the athlete), and establish expectations (attitude, effort, com-mitment, monetary investment). You are still the parent and must guide and influence them through good times and bad. Encourage and lift up! Enjoy the journey!"

—**Bryan and Krista Gerlich** (Athletic Director, Frenship ISD; Texas Tech Women's Basketball Coach)

"Don't go over the top with club and select teams. Your school teams should take precedence over club and select. It should all be about the team, not you."

—**Blake Feldt** (Athletic Director, Midland ISD)

"The full development of an athlete begins with participating in multiple sports. Each sport contributes to the overall develop-ment and success of an athlete both physically and mentally. The development of hand-eye coordination, footwork, and mental and physical toughness can only truly be developed by participating in different sports; each sport complements the others to help develop a better all-around athlete. Participating in different sports most importantly helps athletes avoid burn-out in their favorite or most skilled sport. Overuse of the same muscles and playing hundreds and sometimes thousands of youth games have a negative effect both mentally and physically on the young athlete and leads to the athlete quitting sports altogether in the long run."

—**Rodney Chant** (Executive Director of Athletics, San Angelo ISD)

"As a collegiate athletics administrator as well as the parent of two competitive high school–aged student athletes, I wish the highly competitive teams (e.g., travel, lessons, etc.) did not begin until at least middle school. I have seen many extremely talented student athletes that are completely burned out by the time they reach the collegiate level and quit the sport. Parents should view their financial investment in their children's athletic activities not as investing in a future scholarship but rather as an investment in allowing their child to do something that makes them happy. Parents need to understand that just because they may spend thousands of dollars on lessons, travel ball, club, and more does not entitle their child to make a team or even play a specific position."

—**Scott Larson** (Director of Athletics, Lubbock Christian University)

"If you are looking for college scholarships, other than in football, basketball, and volleyball, they are hard to get and limited. The time and money some spend on kids age six and up on clubs, private lessons, and traveling might very well offset the cost of the athletic scholarship your child probably won't get in the other sports. Additionally, spending time on academics (study habits, completing homework, testing strategies/prep) will most likely offset the missed athletic scholarship. There is so much academic scholarship money out there for students if they just try to really go get it. Sports can help change lives but so can being a successful student. A great coach or professor/teacher can help shape the future of this world. Encourage your child to be well-rounded and productive outside their bubble."

—**Nick Cordes** (Director of Cross Country/Track & Field,
Lubbock Christian University)

"Beyond keeping your children active and healthy, put your kids in competitive athletics so they can learn and benefit from the valuable life lessons athletics teaches us, such as discipline, accountability, mental toughness, teamwork, and how to handle adversity, just to name a few. A college scholarship should be a secondary goal or reason. Only a very small fraction of young athletes will earn a college scholarship, and an even fewer number will earn a scholarship to a Power Five school or have a chance to play professionally. Let your kids fail and learn from it; let them struggle; let them learn to work out problems and to communicate with their teammates and coaches; let them learn to work with people of all walks of life and experiences. The most valuable lesson learned from playing competitive sports is what you do when you work really hard at something and that thing still doesn't go your way. Ironically enough, I learned many of these lessons as a young athlete and continue to have these lessons reinforced in athletics as a coach of over twenty years."

—**Jay Northcutt** (Texas High School Coach)

"Your success as a parent is not predicated on how successful your child is in athletics. Your measuring stick as to how you are doing as a parent should be based on the kind of human your child is—how he treats you, his coaches, teachers, friends, girlfriend, delivery guy, waitress, how he speaks to adults, how he serves, how he cares . . . Your identity as a parent should not be in the sport your kid plays. And parents must model all of these behaviors. Your child wants to hear 'I am proud of you; I love you; let's go get a milkshake.'"

—**Charles "Chuck" Wells** (Texas High School Coach)

"Be their biggest fan, but not their critic or coach. Support them in their understanding of hard work and perseverance, but do not force any of this. If they want to get better, they will, and you can't keep them from it. If they don't, nothing you do can change that, but instead, your efforts to change it will drive them away from the sport. Help them understand that their value has nothing to do with their success, period. Show them this by engaging in conversation and activities outside of athletics too. They need your support, not your pressure. And most importantly, help them understand and respect authority by always supporting coaching decisions (safety issues excluded, of course)."

—**Nathan Blackwood** (Head Baseball Coach, Lubbock Christian University, Texas High School Referee)

"I would like parents to think about their child's long-term future. Is it truly athletic longevity, or is it a lifetime of academic readiness for life? If you ask parents, they probably will say it was all worth the money to watch their child compete and have fun. I agree; I love watching my child in that capacity. However, the endgame and the financial impact of a household to have your kids pay to be on an 'elite' team, to pay for 'elite' private training, to travel the country to go to 'THE' tournament that will get your child seen by college coaches is a waste of money! In my opinion.

"I wish you could take a high school–aged student athlete that has done these things in whatever sport and ask their parents to come up with a financial data sheet on the costs of fees, individual training costs, monthly costs to be on that team, travel expenses, etc. I believe the parents would be completely shocked at what they have spent on *all* the extra things involved with today's youth teams. Then when college comes around, they are totally banking on a scholarship that 'might come through.' When in all reality, that same money invested in a college fund, sending them to an educational tutor to be the best student, or extra time learning to write or read a thought-provoking book could give them the best chance at an amazing life for their family and beyond.

"The bottom line is to give your kids the experience of being on a team and being a great teammate. Just know that your child will be a positive member of society and for their families much longer than they will be an athlete. Make the daily focus on your kid's grades, not how they did at practice or at their game, and make the academic side the priority of the conversation. Encourage them! Regardless of the team, the coach, the ref, or any other factors in the game or on their test scores or class grades, encourage them. Don't find someone to blame; find something to encourage them."

—**Caleb Holt** (Texas High School Coach)

"I have coached and taught for thirty years, and I believe the most important thing for young athletes and parents of those athletes is to let the athlete experience failure and learn through it. Their failures will teach them more about themselves and life instead of adults trying to save them from those. Parents need to be supportive on wins and losses and give them time to digest, on their own, what they learned from each.

"'Let coaches coach, players play, and parents cheer' is the best advice I have heard. Many youths are getting burned out at a young age and having more anxiety from the pressures that parents are putting on them or the pressure the athlete perceives is coming from them. I tell my athletes weekly to 'work hard—have fun!'"

—**Stefani Shortes** (Texas High School Coach)

"Every parent wants their kids to have self-confidence and to be happy, but those can't be given. You have to earn self-confidence. If you have no self-confidence, it's because you have not done anything yet. You have to go try something, fail, learn from it, try again and get better, and then say, 'Look what I was able to do.' A kite can't fly without turbulence. Self-confidence comes from what you did, not from what someone told you you could do. You have to earn being special."

—**Kyle Mickles** (Texas High School Coach)

"Encourage your kids to focus on their present competitive opportunities and not be overwhelmed by their future competitive possibilities. Learn to celebrate your kids' athletic grind, not just their shine. Sowing seeds of hard work today will reap a harvest of competitive commitment and perseverance tomorrow. Teach your kids how to esteem and encourage other players on the team. Being a great teammate is as valuable as being a great player for the team."

—**Ryan Young** (NFL Alumni, NCAA Coach)

"Looking back on my experience as a trampoline and tumbling coach, I would like to share with young athletes that failure is part of the journey. Failure is a beautiful thing because it shows us the human side of ourselves. It's also a good reminder of why we are doing sports in the first place. Because it's fun! To the parents of young athletes, maintaining a balanced life of sports and rest fuels a child's athletic performance. Keep a watchful eye on when your kid is getting spread too thin. As a coach, I have noticed that children bounce back quickly when given time off with family. It really worked for me as a young athlete."

—**Jacob Stephenson** (Trampoline, Tumbling, & Double Mini Coach)

"Athletes: The best measurable attribute you can have is consistency. Show up every day. Just by showing up, you demonstrate a high level of commitment to your coaches and the team. You can't get better if you aren't there. Trust the process. You are important, but you aren't the most important.

"Parents: The best thing you can do for your athlete is to support the coaches. Be a resource and a source of encouragement. Not every athlete is going Division I. Let them enjoy the process. Hold them accountable; don't make excuses for them."

—**Monte Sparkman** (Head Strength & Conditioning Coach, Texas High School Coach)

"There are many things I would love to share with young athletes and parents. I have been both an athlete for many years and now a parent of a young athlete. The biggest thing that I have learned is that sports are *not* that important. In the scheme of life, they are not that important. Do they add value and life lessons and many great experiences? Yes! Absolutely. I do believe, though, that it is essential for young athletes to understand that they are more than their performance on the court, ball field, or arena. How good or not good (by the standards of the world or athletic world) they are or how they perform does not define who they are or their worth. Does God want us to strive for excellence in what our hands find to do? Yes. But a stat sheet, box score, and final record do not tell the whole story. The spirit of an individual is worth more and matters more than what is physically seen.

"I believe that athletes thrive when they are seen as more than just an athlete, when they comprehend that there is more to life than what we see, and when they understand the value of being a great teammate. Selfishness and self-promotion are so prevalent in our culture and society, but that is the opposite of what Christ taught. I believe that we cannot separate our faith from who we are—even in sports. Rather, your faith and walk with Christ will enhance your physical ability that God provided. A true understanding of God and who he is will bring about more passion, drive, and endurance than anyone could imagine.

"I also think that it is important for parents to understand that the performance of their young athlete does not determine nor reflect whether they are a good parent or not. What matters is that their young athlete learns how to be a good teammate and learns what I stated above—sports are not that important. I would also like to share that I love sports, I have been a part of sports for most of my life, but the more I have come to understand who God is and the importance of things outside the realm of what my eyes see, I have come to enjoy and 'succeed' more in the athletic world. Parent–child, athlete–coach, and teammate–teammate relationships can either enrich or starve the joys and experience of athletics. As is true in any endeavor, people matter, and the people you choose to surround yourself and your athlete with matter.

"In conclusion, continuing to understand and value what really matters in life (the unseen world more than the physical world) will spur each individual on to a new level of potential that only God could provide through his design and spirit."

—**Kaycie Wilsom** (NCAA Women's Basketball Coach)

"Parents, if your son or daughter is good at something, push them toward it. Pay no regard to the possibility of a scholarship or professional career in sports. If they are talented enough, those things will take place. Enjoy!"

—**Ged Kates** (Texas High School Coach)

# Student Athlete Words of Wisdom

The following are responses to the question, "What words of wisdom can you share with athletes and parents to help them successfully navigate competitive sports?"

The responses from student athletes validate the need for the information found in this book. More importantly, the responses gave these NCAA student athletes a space to share their private thoughts about their involvement in competitive sport.

The competitive sport landscape has changed. This generation of competitive athletes is contending with much more than performance demands. For example, in 2021 the NCAA passed name, image, and likeness policies and revised transfer portal policies that potentially undermine team dynamics. We, Monica and David, have never lined up against a transgender athlete (a conversation that is layered, emotional, and cannot be addressed adequately in this book). Also, consider the prevalence of social media, and the introduction of player–fan interactions via "mic up" pregame practices. All compounded by a decline in mental and emotional coping skills. The shifting competitive landscape adds pressure to athletics.

Like the "In Their Own Words" section, we list the responses with no changes or context. This is raw data, where the athletes pour out their passions and disclose their experiences for you and your athlete's benefit. Listen, because these student athletes have been there and done that. There is a lot of practical wisdom given by these collegiate athletes. Read, reflect, and be challenged.

"As far as athletes go, when engulfed in the world of competitive sports, it's important to develop a strong work ethic and stay consistent with it, as consistency is what separates the elite athletes from the average. Furthermore, regarding parents, they must provide that support aspect toward their children competing and remain understanding, while still checking to see if their kids are mentally and physically okay throughout each week."

"For me, having a goal to chase has made a world of difference as I've navigated competitive sports. Finding your goal and understanding how 'failing up' toward that goal fits into the whole experience makes dealing with wins, losses, and good or bad days much easier. Celebrate the little wins along the way to your ultimate goal, but don't break down if something doesn't go exactly right in the process."

"Kids that grow up to be athletes are competitive. They want to win; they want to play; they want to succeed. And having parents that are involved in a healthy and supportive way means everything. But when it's time for that season to end, especially if it's 'early' and they could still compete, it's really hard not to feel like a quitter, a failure, or a waste of potential. And it's really helpful in that time for parents to be okay with, and *supportive* of, that decision and know those feelings are being felt by the athlete, so passive-aggressive comments are doubly hurtful and internalized. We know you love us and loved watching us compete, and there's already a fear of disappointing our parents. So being kind and supportive is good. And we're not giving up forever—we still want to compete and will make space for it—it just will look different and that is okay and healthy. Sometimes that is balanced, saying no to something we have loved so much.

"Also, my parents were supportive and loving and awesome, I just know that's not the case for everyone. Sometimes kids are athletes to please their parents, and it isn't okay for a parent to force their children into things so they can live through their kids' life and experiences. Also, sometimes things get tough and it's okay to make sure they're really ready to be finished or if it's just a hard season. But not being ugly is key, because ultimately your kid is their own person and they have to live with the consequences of choosing to stay in a sport or not. Parents don't always see that saying yes to being an athlete may mean saying no to any community outside their team, and if their team isn't great, that's hard. It may mean staying up late to do homework so they can still compete in class. It means missing class and falling behind, getting out of class, and going straight to practice. It's not just game day and it's not just practice. It touches every other thing—weekends, sleep, school, community, meals, personal time, faith. You spend extra free time going to meetings. Even silly things like when you shower. You often can't have a job, but then how do you afford things? You need shadowing hours for grad school, but when do you get them? And not all of this is really as overwhelming in reality as it is in theory. There are good things—teammates, structure, moving your body, competing, learning how to win well and lose well, pushing yourself, discipline, intensity, perspective, thankfulness. It's just a big mixed bag of pros and cons. So it's not an 'easy' choice to play or not for some people."

"Navigating competitive sports can be hard on all parties involved, though in very different ways. For the athletes, their focus is to perform to the best of their abilities, and whether they like it or not, they are trying to make their coaches, teammates, and parents proud of their work. Parents and coaches should keep this in mind when they start to yell at the athletes. Yes, athletes need to be corrected (many times that means getting chewed out), but sometimes the athletes are harder on themselves than anyone else can be. Sometimes they just need to talk it out and have someone be a soundboard. If the discipline is already there in the athlete, then guidance is more so what is needed in many situations. But the athlete must be disciplined enough to fix their own mistakes and take ownership of their actions and mess-ups, not blaming the team, coaches, or anyone else for their own failures and shortcomings."

"Competitive sports can be extremely stressful, but it can be the best time and years of your life. It is important to be committed, stay persistent, and remember that you are playing because you *love* the game. There will be tough, hard days, but whatever work is put in, the outcome is received."

"I think the wisdom needed for athletes and parents of competitive sport can be widespread, but the focus should be on how to mentally prepare for the pressures. As an athlete, it is the most important thing to be ready for your competition mentally even before physically, so learning techniques that work for them can improve performance. As a parent, I would say to let the athlete worry about the competitive side of their sport, because putting added pressure on them is simply making the competition more difficult than it should seem to them."

"Having a high drive to be successful and wanting to better yourself on your own is a common factor in high-performing athletes—and an easier way of helping push that along is to surround yourself with athletes and coaches with that same mindset. Be okay with being uncomfortable (skills-wise) around teammates that are currently better than you—let it fuel you to surpass them while also learning from them. Take serious responsibility for your training if you really want to be the best athlete you can be!"

# How to Be a Good Fan

As those who have been around competitive athletics for some time now, we have seen the very best and worst of fan behavior. I (Fraze) have witnessed a parent run across a football field to yell at their coach, run back to change shirts, and try to repeat the tantrum a second time (I can't make this up). I have witnessed adults being escorted out of athletic venues, get into physical altercations with other fans, and escalate things to the point in which safety was a concern for exiting officials. Hopefully, adults and students know the line we shouldn't cross as fans. In case this knowledge is not known, here is a list of our favorite "don'ts":

* *Don't* . . . use inappropriate language. (Would your grandmother want you to use those words?)
* *Don't* . . . be offensive in your personalization of players, coaches, officials, teams, and others. (Do not talk about a player's family, dating life, failures, or difficult life circumstances.)
* *Don't* . . . talk to others about things you have no control over or expertise in. ("If I was calling plays," "If my

daughter was playing," "If I was playing," "If this ref was not so stupid," etc., ". . . we would be winning").

* *Don't* . . . threaten a player, coach, or official. ("I will meet you after the game" ref-type of threat.)
* *Don't* . . . coach your kid during the game. (Don't call your kid to the fence, side of the track, side of the court, etc., to give them instruction. They have a coach; let them do their job.)

In short, *be classy* in your support of your athlete and team. Oh, and one more thing. Those running and controlling the game (coaches and officials) really don't care about what you have to say about the game.

Fans have a tremendous roll to play in creating an advantage (home and away) in competition. A *tremendous* roll to play. Here is our list of "dos":

* *A good fan* . . . is loud in their support. (They can be heard in the sport arena.)
* *A good fan* . . . is educated. (They know when to be loud and when to be quiet.)
* *A good fan* . . . travels well. (They are present at home games and away games.)
* *A good fan* . . . buys into the traditions. (They know the team rituals, school yells, and traditions during a game.)
* *A good fan* . . . is creative with their support. (They know how to distract during pivotal moments of a competition.)
* *A good fan* . . . stays out of the coaching and official business during a game. (They voice an appropriate reaction but stay on their side of the game.)

* *A good fan* . . . controls their emotions. (Especially when it begins to feel personal, they know when they are about to cross a line and self-regulate.)

Having a good fan base is a tremendous asset to any athlete and team. Especially in a world where fights are being recorded and shared on socials at every level of play, it is imperative for fans to regulate their passion and participation.

If you want to step up your appropriate heckling game, we recommend this resource from a great fan-heckler, El Paso Athletic Hall of Fame member, and SEC official Chris Snead: *The Bleacher Bible (The True Fan's Guide to Better Heckling).*

# Rules for Parents and Athletic Families

The following list of "rules" was a great resource shared with us by Brian Hodnett (Texas High School coach). We found out about this list from his brother Paul, who received the list from Coach Hodnett when his own kids entered the world of competitive athletics. These are too good not to be shared in their unedited form.

1. It's not about the parents, it's about the kids. And it's supposed to be fun!
2. Parents should set the example of sportsmanship and respect to coaches, officials, and the opposing team. The kids are watching.
3. Athletic success does not always show up on the scoreboard. Praise good effort and sportsmanship.
4. Getting a scholarship is not the goal of athletics. Very few athletes play at the college level.
5. Trust the coaches! Especially in front of your child. Once you don't trust or respect the coach in front

of your child, the child won't trust or respect the coach either.

6. Teach teamwork and humility. Learning to be a good winner is just as important as learning to be a good loser.

7. Don't coach from the stands. If you want to help, join the booster club or sign up to host a team meal!

8. Parents should help prepare their child for the path in life. Don't prepare the path for the child.

9. Help your child fail! It's okay to fail. Failure is a part of life, and athletics is a great teacher for overcoming failure and adversity.

10. Society has become soft! Teach toughness. Don't quit because it gets difficult.

11. Know the difference between an injury and something that hurts.

12. Unless it's an emergency, see the trainer before you go to the doctor.

13. Coaches do have favorites; the kids that show up every day, work hard, have a good attitude, make their grades, and stay out of trouble are the favorites.

14. When your child comes home with a story of what happened, there are always two sides to every story. The truth is usually somewhere in the middle.

15. Uncoachable kids turn into unemployable adults.

16. Prepare for life after athletics; at some point, your playing days will end.

17. Don't talk to the coach about playing after the game. Everyone needs some time to cool off before that conversation takes place.

18. Try to build a balanced athlete with physical strength, mental strength, and emotional strength.

19. Don't compare your child's ability and talent to other members of the team, especially in front of your child.
20. The single best thing that a parent can say after the game is "I love watching you play!"

# Five Things to Know before Playing Football

The following "Top Five" lists were collected from middle school, high school, and college coaches. Each have played the game, some at the professional level, and remain involved with the game they love to this day. They were asked the question, "What do young athletes need to know and prepare for as they start their football experience?" Like similar end matter material, because of quality, their words have been recorded as received. Parents, encourage your football athlete to read these words before showing up to their first practice. Parents, read these words and understand what will be expected of your athlete and, in some cases, yourself throughout the football experience.

1. Come prepared. Make sure you have everything you need so you can focus all your attention on football.
2. Make sure you are on time. First impressions are huge. Being late sends a bad message to your coaches and teammates.

3. Make sure your body and mind are in shape and ready for the grind. Work out and get in shape during the off-season.

4. Be prepared to ask questions. If you don't understand something, ask your coach. You don't want to fall behind or not be accountable.

5. Come ready to work. Football is fun, but it demands a lot from you mentally and physically.

> —**Danny McCray** (NFL Alumni Player, Director of the Dallas Cowboy's Youth Football Academy, www.dallascowboys.com, Reality TV personality and Champion)

1. Believe in yourself!

2. Have integrity on and off the field.

3. Control "everything you can control" (don't worry about the rest).

4. Work as hard as you can daily!

5. You don't have to be the best player on the field, but you should try to be the best player you can be (never stop working).

> —**Charles Ali** (NFL Alumni Player, Owner, SHIFT, www.shiftnflflag.com)

Junior High Athletes:

1. Try all sports.

2. Equipment and coaching will be much different from the teams you paid money to play on.

3. Don't get caught up in what team you're put on (A, B, C, etc.). Your body and ability will change while others might already be fully developed.

4. Your teachers will hold you to a higher standard because you are an athlete.

5. Run track!

High School Athletes:

1. Play multiple sports.
2. Set a good impression your freshmen year.
3. Be a student of the game. Watch the sport you play on TV or live.
4. The weight room will make or break you on the playing field.
5. Have fun because most playing careers end after your senior year.

—**Kerry Graham** (Texas High School Coach)

1. Learn to enjoy the process. You will commit so much time and effort to only be guaranteed ten games a season.
2. Be prepared, watch as much film as you can. Being prepared equals confidence.
3. Be on time and don't miss. Seems obvious but you'd be surprised.
4. Have a *why*. Why do you play (what motivates you)?
5. Keep your head down and work. Every year the number of players in your class shrinks.

—**Brandon Roberson** (Texas High School Coach)

Junior High Athletes:

1. Take care of your body (hygiene).
2. Competitive athletics is not a PE class.
3. Realize there is a "structure" to practice. Follow it.
4. Take responsibility in the classroom and in the hallway.
5. There is an increased level of competitiveness. It is not little league anymore.

High School Athletes:

1. Know and accept the time commitment.
2. Know and accept that you will be pushed.
3. Instill in yourself a tough winning attitude.
4. The expectation and seriousness of high school athletics is real.
5. Accept the workload. There is no time for whiners.

—**Noel Ramos** (Texas High School Coach)

1. Be early.
2. Have a positive attitude.
3. Hustle everywhere.
4. Go as hard as you can on every rep.
5. Do more than what's expected.

—**Mark Ribado** (Texas High School Coach, College Head Coach)

Junior High Athletes:

1. Go to your local and area football camps. Find out if your high school feeder offers incoming seventh grade strength and conditioning and go.
2. Know the positions and have an idea of what position you want to play, but be open-minded to be placed in a position by your coach.
3. Practice throwing, catching, snapping, punting, kicking, and running with a football as much as possible.
4. If you want to get noticed, hustle, be physical, be first in drills, run everywhere you go, and look at the coach when he speaks.
5. Don't be the class clown.

High School Athletes:

1. Understand you're a small fish in a big pond and you're gonna have to compete for everything; be coachable.
2. Attend all offered strength and conditioning and football-specific workouts that are provided.
3. Attend all practices and be on time. Make sure you know how the coaches communicate with players and be a part of that.
4. Stay on top of your grades.
5. Show up early for practice so you can get dressed and still have time to get your mind right for practice.

—**Jay Northcutt** (Texas High School Coach)

1. Take a serious approach to academics: NO PASS—NO PLAY. Have positive classroom conduct, effort, and respect for teachers and admin.
2. Trust the decisions of the coach—position, playing time, etc.
3. Be coachable. Understand the coach has you and your team's best interest at heart. See the big picture.
4. If you have a concern, share that with your coach first. Do not go home whining to your parents.
5. Be a team player. Know your role. Not all are super stars—one can still be a positive contributor to the team—BE LOYAL to your team and coaches.

—**David Crume** (Texas High School Coach)

Junior High Athletes:

1. Your momma or dad cannot help you in this endeavor. They may want to try, but it will cause more harm than good.
2. You must stand on your own two feet and deal with it. He may be thirteen and six feet tall already and have a beard, but you must compete with him, and you can.
3. This will be the first time to learn about injury and pain. Pain can play still, and injury can too. How much you can stand will determine how tough you are. Everyone will be in pain, but not everyone will be injured. Go see the coach over injury and not mom, she will have you out for two weeks in a matter of minutes. How much the body can do is amazing, even when the mind is screaming at you to stop. Coach will never ask more of you than you can do.
4. Do not be afraid of your coaches. He may scream and yell at you, but he loves you more than you will ever know. You are his kid.
5. You are not as good as you think you are. You are never as good as mom and dad think you are. But if you work at it, you might be one day. It will take time.

High School Athletes:

1. The mental game is huge, and you must get a grasp of this.
2. A great athlete does not seek admiration; it will find him.
3. Family and relationships are the real gems of athletics. It is what you will remember about sports. They will

be your best friends for life. Sport teaches so much about the family and how it works.

4. No regret when you are done. Either with today's practice or game or season. Give it what it deserves from you.

5. You do not want to win as much as coach does. This is his life and dreams. His paycheck. His family. Remember that when you want to question his actions. He loves you, but not over the team. His decision is based off what is best for the team, not you. It sucks sometimes because of his love for you and wishing you success.

6. It is okay to show emotion; yes, real men cry sometimes. Saying I love you is okay.

—**Bill Rogers** (Texas High School Coach)

# Helpful Verses for Athletes and Families

We were asked to provide a few of our favorite go-to verses regarding sport and personal faith. These verses are helpful to our faith journey, and we hope they are helpful for you as well.

**Anger**

Proverbs 15:1

Proverbs 22:24

Proverbs 30:33

Ecclesiastes 7:9

Ecclesiastes 10:4

Ephesians 4:26

James 1:19–20

**Discipline**

Proverbs 10:17

Proverbs 12:1

Proverbs 15:32

1 Corinthians 9:24

2 Timothy 1:7

Hebrews 12:11

**Family**

Exodus 20:12

Psalms 133:1

Proverbs 6:20

Proverbs 11:29

Proverbs 22:6

Ephesians 6:4

Colossians 3:13, 21

1 Timothy 5:8

3 John 4

## Identity
Matthew 15:17–20
1 Corinthians 6:19–20
2 Corinthians 2:15
2 Corinthians 3:12
Galatians 1:10
Ephesians 2:10
Colossians 3:12
1 Peter 2:9
1 John 3:2

## Mental health
Deuteronomy 31:8
Psalm 18:32
Psalm 34:17
Psalm 40:1–3
Psalm 42:11
Isaiah 41:10
Isaiah 43:1
Jeremiah 29:11
John 14:27
2 Corinthians 1:3–4
Philippians 4:6–7
2 Timothy 1:7
1 John 1:9

## Mindset
Philippians 4:4–20

## Perseverance
Romans 5:1–5

## Physical health
Genesis 1:29
Exodus 15:26
Psalms 139:14
Proverbs 3:5–8
Proverbs 17:22
Proverbs 20:1
Proverbs 31:17
Isaiah 53:5
Mark 11:24
Romans 12:1–2
1 Corinthians 3:16–17
1 Corinthians 6:19–20
1 Corinthians 10:31
Philippians 4:13
1 Timothy 4:8
3 John 2

## Work
Proverbs 14:23
Proverbs 21:25
Colossians 3:23

## Select Proverbs for athletes and families
Proverbs 16:18
Proverbs 16:24
Proverbs 16:28
Proverbs 16:32
Proverbs 17:4
Proverbs 17:14
Proverbs 17:27
Proverbs 22:11

# Helpful Resources

This is a short list of authors and assorted resources that we have used with athletes, coaches, and teams. Some of the names may be familiar. Some are more difficult to read than others. All are helpful and provide further opportunities to learn and grow in your journey through competitive athletics.

**Jon Gordon.** He has written a great deal around the topic of team building and athletic development. We recommend his classics *Energy Bus* and *The Power of a Positive Team*. A great set of books for anyone.

**Jon Gordon and Damon West.** The two collaborated on the book *The Coffee Bean*. This book is a focused expansion on Damon West's first book, *The Change Agent*. Both books are great reads and are instantly applicable to competitive athletes.

*Jon Gordon and Mike Smith.* The two collaborated to create a powerful book on team dynamics, *You Win in the Locker Room First*. A great book for coaches and team captains.

***Jocko Willink and Leif Babin.*** This pair of authors served in the Navy Seals together and bring the lessons they learned about team leadership and personal development to the reader in powerful and engaging fashion. Their resources continue to expand, but we suggest starting with *Extreme Ownership* and *The Dichotomy of Leadership*. A great set of books for both athlete and coach.

**Dr. Nate Zinsser.** Dr. Zinsser trains on mental toughness at the West Point Military Academy and is the author of *The Confident Mind*. The concepts have been translated into athletic performance by players such as Eli Manning, who profited from Dr. Zinsser's training. A great book for anyone wanting practical guidance in building mental self-talk and strength.

***James Clear.*** Clear's book *Atomic Habits* has made a big splash in performance literature. In short, small (atomic) changes lead to big changes. Another great book for anyone wanting to make changes in their life.

***Damon West and Stephen Mackey.*** West and Mackey have produced a great resource for team dynamics in *The Locker Room*. This award-winning resource is great for both coach and athlete.

**Todd G. Gongwer.** *Lead . . . for God's Sake!* is a great book, told as a parable, on leadership. This book is a great starting place for coaches wanting to understand and take the leadership of their team to the next level.

***Eric Thomas.*** "The Hip-Hop Preacher" works with the MLB, NFL, NBA, Nike, Under Armour, Fortune 500 Companies, and others. Thomas takes a "common-sense approach to living a successful, satisfying professional and personal life" in any industry at any level (https://ericthomas.com/category/about/).

***Inky Johnson.*** This former football player offers helpful tips on life, mental agility, change, leadership, teamwork, and excelling in struggles (https://www.inkyjohnson.com/).

***Kobe Bryant.*** Kobe Bryant's book *Mamba Mentality: How I Play* is about focus and commitment to a goal. It is a book about mental toughness needed for focus. See also, Tyler Brandt, "Mamba Mentality: The Mindset that Made Kobe Bryant a Master," Fee Stories, January 30, 2020, https://fee.org/articles/mamba-mentality-the-mindset-that-made-kobe-bryant-a-master/.

***Dr. Ken Ravizza and Dr. Tom Hanson.*** *Heads Up Baseball 2.0* is a great read, and it serves as an early effort to consolidate mental skills training into a manual-style book. This book offers coaches, players, and parents a resource to support mental-skills development for common challenges athletes face. These challenges may include fear, lack of confidence, anxiety, arousal, and mental rehearsal.

**Dr. Robert Weinberg and Dr. Daniel Gould.** *Foundations of Sport and Exercise Psychology* is the most widely used textbook in sport and exercise psychology. The book offers research, case studies, and practical applications for psychological and mental skills training. Some of the areas covered in the book pertain to motivation, goal setting, burnout, injury, aggression, personality constructs, and youth sport.

# NOTES

## Introduction

[1] Michael Phelps, "Michael Phelps Opens Up about His Struggles with Mental Health | Outside the Lines," interview by Jeremy Schaap, YouTube video, 5:38, May 18, 2020, https://www.youtube.com/watch?v=gea6 HOo6ZEM.

[2] Kevin Love, "Kevin Love Details His Battles with Mental Illness | ESPN," interview by Jackie MacMullan, YouTube video, 5:37, August 20, 2018, https://www.youtube.com/watch?v=k-ov9XZzByA.

[3] "Simone Biles Withdraws from Women's All-Around Final," Olympics, July 28, 2021, https://olympics.com/en/news/simone-biles-withdraws-from -women-s-all-around-final.

[4] "All I Do Is Win," featuring T-Pain, Ludacris, Snoop Dogg, and Rick Ross, MP3 audio, track 3 on DJ Khaled, *Victory*, We the Best and E1, 2010.

## Balance Matters

[1] Some reading this book may be involved in private or Homeschool Alliance athletics and feel balance is not a concern for their student athlete in that Sundays and Wednesdays are still "sacred." Perhaps these days will remain so, but balance is always something parents and athletes should be vigilant in protecting.

[2] The practice of Sabbath is seen throughout the Scriptures. To most readers, the practice of Sabbath has been understood as going to church on Sundays. However, the practice of Sabbath is much more than participation in a worship assembly. Indeed, like the Creator, his creation must rest or quickly fall out of balance.

[3] Robert S. Weinberg and Daniel Gould, *Foundations of Sport and Exercise Psychology*, 7th ed. (Champaign, IL: Human Kinetics, 2019).

[4] Ronald B. Woods, *Social Issues in Sport*, 3rd ed. (Champaign, IL: Human Kinetics, 2016).

## Coaching Matters

[1] Instead of giving you one or two researched articles (which you probably would not read), the authors suggest searching the phrase, "What effects do yelling coaches have on athletes? research articles," on the internet. There are plenty of sources highlighting the damage coaches (and parents) can have on athlete performance and mental health.

[2] For example, if a gymnast falls off a balance beam and the coach says, "Don't fall," the athlete is concentrating on not falling and will, more than likely, fall. But if the fall is followed by positive words—"Keep your eyes focused on your mark"—the athlete will concentrate on that mark and, more than likely, correct that which is creating the fall. This quality is why a coach hands the ball off quickly again to the same running back that just fumbled the football.

## Conflict Matters

[1] Plato, *The Dialogues of Plato*, trans. B. Jowett, vol. 3 (New York: Charles Scribner's Sons, 1908), 118.

[2] "Resolution" is a loaded word. It does not imply that there are no consequences given or suffered from sinful or hurtful actions. It does mean that some level of appropriate relationship has been restored. The resources given in this chapter will assist in further explaining healthy resolution.

[3] Both of these practical practices for conflict can be found in James 1:19–21 and Galatians 6:2–5.

[4] These are a few of my favorite resources on conflict management: *Helping People Forgive*, by David W. Augsburger; *Controlling the Costs of Conflict: How to Design a System for Your Organization*, by Karl A. Slaikeu and Ralph H. Hasson; *Church Conflict: The Hidden Systems behind the Fights*, by Charles H. Cosgrove and Dennis D. Hatfield; *Meeting the Moment: Leadership and Well-Being in Ministry*, by G. Douglas Lewis; *When Push Comes to Shove: A Practical Guide to Mediating Disputes*, by Karl A. Slaikeu; *Managing the Congregation: Building Effective Systems to Serve People*, by Norman Shawchuck and Roger Heuser; and *Managing Church Conflict*, by Hugh F. Halverstadt.

[5] This verse has nothing to do with the worship assembly. It has to do with reconciliation.

[6] To get a great understanding of systems and how they function in a church, work through *Generation to Generation: Family Process in Church and Synagogue*, by Edwin H. Friedman.

[7] A withdrawal is not avoidance. Withdrawal indicates that a time-out has been called to settle emotions and that a promise has been made to resume discussion at a later date. Because a student's playing time can be impacted, this step is not preferable. Still, some sort of emotional withdrawal is critical to manage conflict.

[8] Search "conflict style inventory" and you will find a number of assessments. Caution: As with all things Internet, there are a number of free inventories that may or may not be legitimate.

[9] Read the end matter and the chapter "Strength and Conditioning Matters" for the reasoning behind our opinion and direction.

[10] It has been our experience that toxic coaches or programs are able to stay when winning is more important than "how" you win. It these situations, it is sad what a parent and community will put up with, compromise, and sacrifice in character to secure the title of *champion*.

## Failure Matters

[1] This truth is common knowledge and easy to verify. Failure's relationship to growth is part of all the high-level athletic programs the authors have been associated with.

[2] Consider the popular statement inspired by Thomas Edison's words: "I have not failed 700 times. I have succeeded in proving that those 700 ways will not work. When I have eliminated the ways that will not work, I will find the way that will work." That is a constructive use of "failure." "Thomas Edison Inventing the Light Bulb—Entrepreneurs' Must Read," DCD Agency, June 27, 2012, https://dcdagency.com/thomas-edison-inventing-the-light-bulb-entrepreneurs-must-read.

[3] David Fraze and Walter Surdacki, *Practical Wisdom for Youth Group Parents: Parnering with Your Youth Minister* (Abilene, TX: Leafwood Publishers, 2022).

[4] A student's athletic failure will hurt your heart but should not be taken personally and embarrass you. If it does, ask yourself why it embarrasses you and dive into the root of that dysfunction. I use the word *necessarily* because, in some situations, the pressure a parent places on a student athlete's performance may indeed lead to failure in execution.

## Fun Matters

[1] Kyle Idleman, *Not a fan: Becoming a Completely Committed Follower of Jesus* (Michigan: Zondervan, 2011), 24–25.

[2] Woods, *Social Issues in Sport*, 6.

[3] Jay Coakley, *Sports in Society: Issues and Controversies*, 12th ed. (New York: McGraw-Hill, 2016).

[4] At the highly competitive school Dr. Fraze works with in Texas, "fun" is spoken of frequently by coaches, valued, and a key element in the athletic culture.

[5] Dr. Ivan Joseph, "The Skill of Self Confidence," TEDx Talks, YouTube, January 13, 2012, https://www.youtube.com/watch?v=w-HYZv6HzAs&t=9s.

[6] "Values, Victory, and Peace of Mind Present the Greatest Coach of the 20th Century—Coach John Wooden," YouTube video, accessed February 22, 2016, https://www.youtube.com/watch?v=DtaaVEZFYqk; John Wooden and Steve Jamison, "The Pyramid of Success," John Wooden Coach and Teacher, accessed February 29, 2016, http://www.coachwooden.com /pyramid-of-success; "Wooden's Pyramid of Success: A Philosophy that Produced Extraordinary Results," The John R. Wooden Course, accessed March 15, 2016, http://www.woodencourse.com/woodens_wisdom.html.

## Identity Matters

[1] Ronda Rousey, "Ronda Rousey Discusses Her UFC Upset," interview with Ellen DeGeneres, YouTube video, 6:17, February 16, 2016, https://www .youtube.com/watch?v=iwCdv9iR8P8.

[2] Britton Brewer, Judy Van Raalte, and Darwyn Linder, "Athletic Identity: Hercules' Muscles or Achilles' Heel?," *International Journal of Sport Psychology* 24, no. 2 (1993): 237–54.

[3] Michael Phelps, "Michael's Mental Health Story," Michael x Talkspace, https://www.talkspace.com/michael.

[4] Weinberg and Gould, *Foundations of Sport and Exercise Psychology*.

[5] Woods, *Social Issues in Sport*, 6.

[6] Matt Stepp, "10 Most Attended TXHSFB Games of All-Time," Texas Football, December 26, 2021, https://www.texasfootball.com/article/2021 /12/26/10-most-attended-txhsfb-games-of-all-time?ref=related_title.

[7] Márcio Domingues, "Growth and Functional Development in 6 to 10 Year Old Soccer Players: Constraints and Possibilities," *Annals of Applied Sport Science* 1, no. 4 (Winter 2013): 5–16.

[8] Maxine Morrison and David Weicker, eds., "Long Term Athlete Development," Athletics Canada, https://athletics.ca/wp-content/uploads /2015/01/LTAD_EN.pdf.

## Mindset Matters

[1] *Mindsets*, especially fixed and growth mindsets, are prevalent in discussions of both athletic and cognitive development and performance. A great starting place for definitions can be found in a simple web search.

[2] Here are a few of the books that have been helpful to me on the topic of mindset. Again, this is only a sampling. *The Confident Mind: A Battle-Tested Guide to Unshakable Performance*, by Nate Zinsser; *Atomic Habits: An Easy and Proven Way to Build Good Habits and Break Bad Ones*, by James Clear; *Overthinking: Control Your Thoughts, Think Positive, and Master Your Mindset*, by Gary Hill; *The Infinite Game*, by Simon Sinek; and *Extreme Ownership: How U.S. Navy SEALs Lead and Win*, by Jocko Willink and Leif Babin.

[3] For more details of the Titanic's tragic end, see Sarah Pruitt, "Why Did the Titanic Sink?," History Channel, updated June 29, 2023, https://www.history.com/news/why-did-the-titanic-sink.

## Parenting Matters

[1] John O'Sullivan, "The Ride Home," Changing the Game Project, May 1, 2014, https://changingthegameproject.com/the-ride-home-after-the-game; Christina Callaway, "The Car Ride Home: Why So Many Kids Quit," Coach Up Nation, October 30, 2017, http://www.coachup.com/nation/articles/the-car-ride-home-why-so-many-kids-quit?gad_source=1&gclid=EAIaIQobChMI4qPL5ofXgwMVyCqtBh1hlgGTEAAYASAAEgIpi_D_BwE.

[2] Nick Buonocore, "The Car Ride Home," Reformed Sports Project, March 18, 2022, https://reformedsportsproject.com/blog/f/the-car-ride-home?blogcategory=Mental+Health.

[3] Rick Wolff, *Good Sports: The Concerned Parent's Guide to Competitive Youth Sports*, 2nd ed. (Champaign, IL: Sagamore, 1997).

[4] See "Parent's Role in Youth Sports," National Academy of Athletics, accessed February 7, 2024, https://nationalacademyofathletics.com/parents-role-in-youth-sports/.

[5] "*The Art of Learning*, Josh Waitzkin—Book Summary," *Zen Flowchart* (blog), May 9, 2023, https://www.zenflowchart.com/blog/the-art-of-learning-josh-waitzkin-book-summary; Patrick Egan, "*The Art of Learning*: Four Principles from Josh Waitzkin's Book," *Educational Renaissance* (blog), February 22, 2020, https://educationalrenaissance.com/2020/02/22/the-art-of-learning-four-principles-from-josh-waitzkins-book/.

[6] Eduardo Briceno, "The Power of Belief: Mindset and Success," TEDx Talks, YouTube, November 18, 2012, https://www.youtube.com/watch?v=pN34FNbOKXc.

## Reality Matters

[1] To be clear, he did not doubt the power and all-consuming grace of God. It appears one of the greatest threats to Paul's confidence was the discouragement that came from his memory of past failure and the consequences of persecuting Christ followers. I find this a rather human response and struggle that should be a comfort and encouragement to all who struggle with their past failures and consequences.

[2] If indeed there is a conflict with a coach, organization, or trainer, please consult the chapters "Conflict Matters" and "Coaching Matters" before the meeting.

[3] This false reality has been witnessed by the authors firsthand and is often discussed openly by coaches who receive pressure from families that have been told their student athlete has the ability to play at the "next level" if coached correctly.

[4] "Estimated Probability of Competing in College Athletics," NCAA, last updated April 8, 2020, https://www.ncaa.org/sports/2015/3/2/estimated-probability-of-competing-in-college-athletics.aspx; "Varsity Odds," Scholarship Stats, https://scholarshipstats.com/varsityodds; "NCAA Recruiting Facts," NCAA, August 2014, https://www.nfhs.org/media/886012/recruiting-fact-sheet-web.pdf.

## Responsibility Matters

[1] Weinberg and Gould, *Foundations of Sport and Exercise Psychology*.

## Strength and Conditioning Matters

[1] Monica J. Williams, "Moderator Effect of Competitive Levels on Athletic Identity and Conduct in Sport" (PhD diss., Grand Canyon University, 2022), https://www.proquest.com/openview/77afd9b47013b240ec3709e7ee62f4a6/1?pq-origsite=gscholar&cbl=18750&diss=y; Davis L. Rogers, Miho J. Tanaka, Andrew J. Cosgarea, Richard D. Ginsburg, and Geoffrey M. Dreher, "How Mental Health Affects Injury Risk and Outcomes in Athletes," *Sports Health* (2023): doi: 10.1177/19417381231179678.

[2] Sofien Fekih, Mohamed Sami Zguira, Abdessalem Koubaa, Liwa Masmoudi, Nicola Luigi Bragazzi, and Mohamed Jarraya, "Effects of Motor Mental Imagery Training on Tennis Service Performance during the Ramadan Fasting: A Randomized, Controlled Trial," *Nutrients* 12, no. 4

(April 2020): 1035, https://www.ncbi.nlm.nih.gov/pmc/articles/PMC7231086; Joel Pearson, Thomas Naselaris, Emily A. Holmes, and Stephen M. Kosslyn, "Mental Imagery: Functional Mechanisms and Clinical Applications," *Trends in Cognitive Sciences* 19, no. 10 (Fall 2015): 590–602, https://www.ncbi.nlm.nih.gov/pmc/articles/PMC4595480/.

[3] Nadja Walter, Lucie Nikoleizig, and Dorothee Alfermann, "Effects of Self-Talk Training on Competitive Anxiety, Self-Efficacy, Volitional Skills, and Performance: An Intervention Study with Junior Sub-Elite Athletes," *Sports (Basel)* 7, no. 6 (June 2019): 148. doi: 10.3390/sports7060148.

[4] "7 Tips for Recovering Mentally after a Sports Injury," *Henry Ford Health* (blog), June 21, 2019, https://www.henryford.com/blog/2019/06/7-tips-recovery-after-sports-injury.

## Transition Matters

[1] Most athletes entered sports to have fun with friends and were interested in other activities outside of sports. Those other interests and activities were critical in shaping the whole identity of the individual and instrumental to maintaining the balance needed to combat identity foreclosure and singular-identity development. The "Balance Matters" chapter notes the challenge of finding balance between competitive athletics and spiritual growth. The balance challenges can be extended to include competitive sports and identity.

[2] Jade M. Bell, Steven Prewitt, Vipa Bernhardt, and Dean Culpepper, "The Relationship of Athlete Identity and Career Exploration and Engagement of NCAA Division II Athletes," *International Journal of Exercise Science* 11, no. 5, (2018): 493–502, https://digitalcommons.wku.edu/ijes/vol11/iss5/10/. This article focuses on the correlation between athlete identity and career exploration among DII athletes, but the literature has a broader application to athletes at any level given the presence of athlete identity and its implications of investment in other interests outside of sport.

[3] These references each address factors related to athletic foreclosure, athletic identity, athletic maintenance, and the challenges associated with each for an individual's development of other interests, skills, and talents: Britton W. Brewer and Allen E. Cornelius, "Norms and Factorial Invariance of the Athletic Identity Measurement Scale (AIMS)," *Academic Athletic Journal* 15, no. 2 (2001): 103–13; Britton W. Brewer and Albert J. Petitpas, "Athletic Identity Foreclosure," *Current Opinion in Psychology* 16 (2017): 118–22, https://doi.org/10.1016/j.copsyc.2017.05.004; Britton Brewer, Judy Van Raalte, and Darwyn Linder, "Athletic Identity: Hercules' Muscles or Achilles' Heel?," *International Journal of Sport Psychology* 24, no. 2 (1993):

237–54; Alan J. Good, Britton W. Brewer, Albert J. Petitpas, Judy Van Raalte, and Matthew T. Mahar, "Identity Foreclosure, Athletic Identity, and College Sports Participation," *The Academic Athletic Journal* 8 (1993): 1–13.

## Church Matters

[1]"Intergenerational" refers to actual interaction and activity, not just proximity.

[2]Because of its relevance, most of the "Why?" section has been taken from David Fraze, *Practical Wisdom for Youth Ministry: The Not-So-Simple Truths That Matter* (Abilene, TX: Leafwood Publishers, 2018), 42–44.

[3]More practical wisdom can be found in "Balance Matters."

[4]You can find your area FCA representative by going to www.fca.org.